IN SEARCH OF MONET

IN SEARCH OF MONET

An AI-Assisted Inquiry into Artistic Recognition and Visual Structure

Gary Pierce

Published by Visual Structure Press

wargametech.com/insearchofmonet

Paperback ISBN: 979-8-9962210-1-1
First edition

TABLE OF CONTENTS

PREFACE

An Inquiry Under Constraint

This book records an investigation conducted at the intersection of art and computer-based analysis of digital images. The question of authorship, that is, who painted the works represented by the Study Images, lies outside the scope of this work.

The inquiry is concerned instead with what may be tested when attention is confined strictly to the visible image itself, apart from external records, ownership history, or historical framing. Its purpose is to determine which computational methods can be relied upon to assess specific visual features such as texture, color, and structural pattern under controlled and repeatable conditions.

A work of art exceeds pixels and digital data. For that reason, a clear distinction is maintained throughout between computational analysis and traditional art-historical interpretation. At the same time, the disciplined application of computational methods to visual features may contribute meaningfully to other forms of analysis, provided its limits are clearly defined and carefully observed.

The investigation developed gradually. Early phases were devoted to understanding the capabilities and constraints of the tools employed. Initial assumptions were formed, tested, and frequently revised. Some approaches proved unsuitable and were discarded. Methods were reset, and conditions were tightened. These restarts are preserved as part of the record, as they demonstrate how control was established in practice.

In later stages, emphasis shifted toward stability and repeatability, so that identical methods would yield consistent results under identical conditions. Constraint, in this sense, is not merely a guiding principle but the governing condition of the inquiry.

Artificial intelligence and related computational tools appear throughout as instruments of investigation. Their value depends upon disciplined use. While such tools can produce results quickly, those results carry weight only when they can be reproduced consistently under controlled conditions.

What follows is a record of an investigation conducted within fixed boundaries. It traces a process of repeated testing, revision, and increasing restraint.

From the outset, a stopping condition governed the work. If contradictions emerged under testing, the inquiry would end. Such contradictions would weaken the central question, which asks whether the Study Images align with Claude Monet's style under the defined conditions of image-based analysis.

The analyses presented here show what detailed inspection of the image alone was able to reveal, where patterns remained stable, and where the inquiry reached its natural conclusion. Beyond that point, interpretation belongs to other methods and other forms of evidence.

These pages record only what was established within the scope set for this inquiry.

The full experimental record, including parameter configurations, repeated trials, and extended outputs, is preserved within the “entries” included at the conclusion of each chapter.

The entries follow the chapter structure of this work, with individual entries corresponding to specific phases of the inquiry.

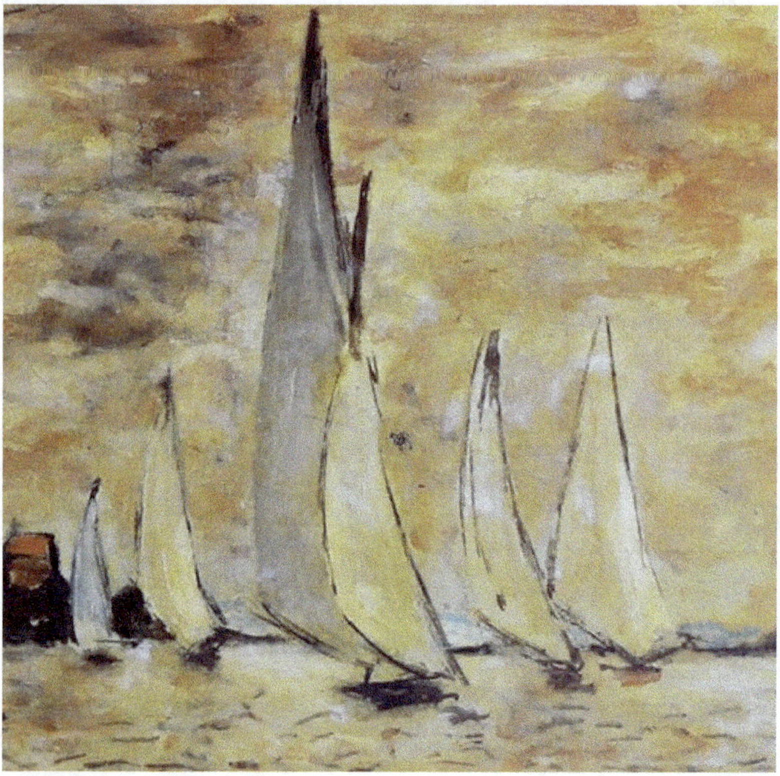

One Image, One Question

Part I

Conditions and Early Structural Formation

CHAPTER 1

Learning Toward a Question

The inquiry began with a problem that resisted resolution: the Study Image bore a strong resemblance to a particular work of Claude Monet. While this initial observation suggested a possible connection, the work did not proceed by assuming or asserting that conclusion. Instead, the image was examined systematically, and any determination was allowed to emerge only through testing and analysis.

The author began this work without formal training in art history. His background was instead in technical fields, including algorithm design, data analysis, statistics, and software development. To explore what it might mean to identify a painting digitally as "by Monet," he had to start from the beginning. This meant learning how art is described, how visual questions are approached, how artificial intelligence can both help and mislead, how to apply logical reasoning to uncertain material, and how to continually revisit assumptions as the work progressed.

For that reason, the methods used in this investigation were not fully formed at the start. They developed as the work progressed. Some early ideas proved useful and were refined, while others were revised or set-aside. As the structure of the inquiry became clearer, more attention was given to the assumptions behind it, to areas of weakness, and to reducing the space where errors might remain.

The main goal was straightforward: to test the method thoroughly and see whether it could produce reliable and consistent results.

At the same time, the inquiry was governed by a stopping rule. If the features observed in the Monet reference material failed to appear in the Study Images under the same conditions, the examination would end. That rule was established in advance, and it gave the inquiry a defined point of termination.

The length of this book reflects the fact that, within that rule, the observed patterns continued to hold.

The Study Image and the Question of Recognition

Two terms govern the pages that follow. "inquiry" refers to the question under examination and to the effort undertaken in response to it. "Study Images" refers to the digital images taken from the unidentified subject. These are the materials examined in this inquiry.

Keeping these terms separate helps make the reasoning easier to follow. The inquiry defines the process, and the Study Images are the materials under examination.

The word "testing" is used here in a specific way. It means applying limits and pressure to see where a method begins to break down. A method should be able to hold up under that pressure. Where it does not, the failure should be clearly visible in the results.

At its core, the inquiry asked whether image-based analysis could consistently detect meaningful differences in physical or visual structure. The work focused on cropped portions of the Study Image, compared against reference patterns associated with Claude Monet.

In the absence of firm documentary context, paintings are often judged by style or left unresolved. This inquiry instead asked whether recognition itself could be examined under controlled conditions.

Calibrating Artificial Intelligence

Artificial intelligence was introduced early in the process. When asked about features commonly associated with Monet, such as light and color, the system responded quickly and with apparent confidence. Its answers often sounded detailed, persuasive, and complete.

That early experience shaped how AI was used going forward. Its responses were treated with caution. If it suggested a similarity, that suggestion was examined. Doing so required clear boundaries. These included what counted as a result, how results would be measured, and how far interpretation could go.

Throughout this book, artificial intelligence is treated as an instrument. It assisted in the exploration of patterns and in statistical data comparison at greater speed. Decisions of direction, judgment, and meaning remained human responsibilities. AI outputs were kept only when they aligned with direct observation and remained within the boundaries set for the inquiry.

Les Barques, Régates à Argenteuil as a Comparison

Before recognition could be examined reliably, a dependable point of comparison was required. Attention therefore turned first to *Les Barques, Régates à Argenteuil* (1874), a painting widely accepted as a work by Monet. The inquiry used a small set of controlled digital crops taken from a high quality reproduction sourced through Getty Images. These crops were extracted and kept separate from the broader Monet reference group. In the initial stages of testing, they served as controlled comparisons.

Expanding the Reference Set

In the earlier phases of the inquiry, one of the central difficulties lay in understanding image quality and the many ways in which it could affect a result. Before broader testing could proceed, it was necessary to learn what qualities a digital image would need in order to support reliable analysis. An early part of the inquiry was learning what was needed before testing could move forward with confidence.

Artists vary within their own body of work. Style can shift over time. Paintings themselves change as they age. Photographs of paintings may alter in color and light according to the conditions under which they are taken. Digital files may introduce further distortions through compression, poor resolution, or other forms of degradation.

For these reasons, digital material was handled with particular care. Resolution, color adjustment, cropping, and compression were controlled as closely as possible to maintain consistency.

Later in the analysis, the reference image sets were expanded. More paintings associated with Monet were added, together with works by non-Monet artists. In its earlier state, the Monet reference material comprised roughly one hundred Monet images. In later chapters, that number grew to several hundred. The non-Monet comparison set also began modestly, with a handful of images by artists such as Van Gogh, Cézanne, Manet, and Renoir. In time, it expanded to include works by a wide range of artists, spanning from the Impressionist period to the present.

The next chapter establishes how subsequent reference images are handled and used. As the inquiry approached completion, the image-based analysis produced a hardened dataset prepared for final analysis.

Entry 01

Entry 01

Book Reference: Chapter 1
Date: 21 January 2025
Phase: Conceptual Exploration of Monet's Artistic Techniques

Objective:

This entry documents the learning completed to build an art historical foundation for the later technical work.

Procedures Completed:

A detailed review was conducted of Monet's key techniques, with attention to his use of color, brushwork, and the handling of reflections on water. His compositional structure was examined, particularly the representation of light in paintings from the Argenteuil period. The historical context of this period and its influence on Impressionism was also studied to ensure the inquiry remained grounded in period practice.

This phase identified specific visual features that could later be tested using computational methods. Brushstroke patterns, tonal relationships, reflections, and overall texture organization were cataloged as testable elements. This work established a bridge between traditional art analysis and the later image-based pipeline by translating descriptive observations into measurable features.

Testing Conducted:

No formal computational testing was conducted at this stage. The work remained preparatory, focusing on research gathering, early conceptual modeling, and outlining how AI and image analysis might detect and compare Monet's surface behavior and visual structure.

Artifacts Produced:

Artifacts included an art historical research compilation with notes on Monet's style and methods, a preliminary framework for visual feature analysis, and a structured list of key visual elements to test, including brushstroke structure, color distribution, tonal relationships, and texture organization. Conceptual summaries were also prepared to outline the intended digital analysis framework.

Status:

This phase concluded with the inquiry positioned for the next stage. Foundational research and conceptual modeling were completed, enabling the transition into computational testing in subsequent entries.

CHAPTER 2

Image Quality as a Precondition

Before testing could begin, the inquiry needed to determine whether the Study Images and the assembled reference material were clear, consistent, and stable enough to support comparison.

This required high-quality digital reproductions that preserve the original works with sufficient fidelity for close analysis. Where a reproduction is blurred, heavily compressed, or uneven in quality, too little dependable detail remains for the analysis to proceed reliably. Further work depended on the stability of the underlying material.

These reproductions needed to preserve the features on which this kind of examination depends: overall structure, the balance of light and dark, edge behavior, color relationships, and composition. When such features are weakened or obscured, confidence in any later result is reduced from the outset.

Resolution and Structural Parity

Resolution was treated as a basic requirement. As visual material was assembled, including the Study Images, Monet references, and non-Monet comparisons, differences in size, clarity, and usable detail became evident. Some images were high in resolution, while others varied considerably in quality. This unevenness posed an immediate difficulty. The working assumption was straightforward: if one group contained more recoverable visual information than another, the comparison would already be inclined in that direction from the start.

Materials falling below the chosen threshold of quality were excluded, even when they appeared promising. The rule was simple: an image was not to gain an advantage merely by carrying more pixels.

Format Stability, Cropping, and Image Integrity

File format also mattered. Some formats preserve information with minimal change. Others compress more aggressively and introduce visible artifacts. Such artifacts can generate textures or edges that do not belong to the original art work.

Compressed files were therefore examined thoroughly. If a resemblance emerged only after heavy compression, it was treated cautiously. A pattern that strengthens as quality declines offers weak ground for trust.

Cropping introduced a different difficulty. A partial view can make certain features appear more pronounced than they are. Once the wider field is removed, proportion and balance can shift. For that reason, cropping was handled with strict control. At this point, it mainly served as a check: a way to see if the features that seemed distinctive still stood out when separated from the whole image, or if they were only noticeable because of the tighter frame.

The files also required careful handling. Basic checks confirmed that they remained unchanged once they entered the project. Once a file was admitted into the working set, it stayed fixed, without casual re-saving or incidental edits. What entered the analysis was expected to remain the same throughout.

Artificial Intelligence in the Preparatory Phase

Artificial intelligence was used frequently during this stage. It raised practical issues concerning resolution, capture quality, compression, and cropping. It also helped organize the working material and track what had already been checked. Its suggestions were considered carefully and kept only when they aligned with direct inspection.

Establishing the Baseline

This stage laid the foundation for placing the material into a condition where later testing could proceed fairly and repeatably. This baseline was established as the starting point and defined what counted as an acceptable file, which crops could be compared, and the minimum handling rules that had to be followed to keep the focus on the material itself. At the heart of this foundation was one steady principle: quality sets the upper limit of what later analysis can support.

By the end of this stage, the rules were clearer, the material was organized, and a baseline had been established to which the inquiry could refer.

The next chapter transitioned into a more exploratory period, with settings allowed to vary so the system's behavior could be observed and the testing capabilities that had been researched put into practice before tighter controls were applied.

Entry 02

Entry 02

Book Reference: Chapter 2
Date: 31 January 2025
Phase: Image Quality & Dataset Preparation

Objective:

This entry documents the steps taken to formalize image admissibility and quality control prior to analytical comparison.

Procedures Completed:

Clear criteria were established for acceptable image quality, including minimum resolution thresholds, compression and artifact checks, and consistent cropping protocols. The full digital corpus was reviewed for structural consistency across the Study Images, the Monet reference set, and the non-Monet controls to ensure that later results would not depend on uneven inputs.

Resolution thresholds were defined for different use cases, separating general viewing from structural comparison and from close surface inspection. These thresholds provided a controlled framework for how images would be evaluated and compared in subsequent phases.

Testing Conducted:

Testing in this phase focused on whether the image set could withstand routine digital processing without altering measurable surface signals. Resolution was evaluated at multiple levels: 2000 × 2000 pixels for general viewing, 4000 × 4000 pixels for structural comparison, and a higher-than-10,000-pixel tier noted as outside the inquiry's scope for close surface inspection.

Compression robustness was tested through recompression at different quality settings, comparisons between JPEG and PNG outputs, lossless versus lossy format checks, and pixel-level difference inspection. Mild blur, sharpening, and denoising sensitivity checks were performed to determine whether common processing adjustments could distort measurable structure.

Cropping and alignment sensitivity were also assessed using geometric transformations and edge-map comparisons to confirm that minor shifts in framing did not introduce artificial differences.

Artifacts Produced:

Artifacts included documented image quality standards, resolution thresholds, compression robustness procedures, and integrity verification methods. Evaluation records were maintained for format comparisons, compression trials, and resolution checks, along with a defined set of admissibility criteria governing inclusion in the analytical dataset.

Status:

This phase concluded with the image corpus formally validated for downstream analysis. The dataset was confirmed to be stable, consistent, and auditable prior to the initiation of interpretive testing.

CHAPTER 3

Exploration to Discipline

This chapter transitions into an exploratory phase, where artificial intelligence and more adaptable tools are used for hands-on testing. The objective was to configure and run several tests to gain a deeper understanding of how the tools function and to observe how the system distinguishes the Study Image from the broader set of images related to Monet's style.

The settings across the entire analytical process were intentionally varied. This included adjustments to image size, crop boundaries, processing steps, and the feature and similarity settings used in the analysis. The goal was to understand which choices had a significant impact, which ones had minimal effect, and which ones led to results that could not be relied upon.

Exploration Under Loose Controls

Early runs often produced patterns that appeared orderly and persuasive. The Study Images frequently appeared close to Monet references within the shared feature space. As visual features were converted into numerical representations, this relationship persisted, with the Study Images clustering near Monet references in the resulting structure. Distance measures were used to quantify the proximity between images in that space. In several runs, when the system measured how similar images were, some Study Images and some Monet images ended up very close to each other numerically.

To make the pattern easier to see, the high-dimensional data was projected into a two-dimensional plot. This projection simplifies the underlying structure but can reveal whether points group together or spread more broadly. In these early runs, the points tended to form orderly clusters rather than a loose scatter.

These early findings were treated as signs of the system's sensitivity. At this stage, strong structure could appear simply because the settings remained flexible.

Artificial intelligence played an active role during this period. The system could generate structured language and propose interpretations that sounded convincing. Without caution, those proposals risked drawing the inquiry toward conclusions the analysis was not yet prepared to support.

AI Collaboration
Computational testing framed as conclusive: Dismissed.

AI Output
Proposed validation of authenticity through brushstroke, spectral, and machine learning analysis.

Author's Note
Authentication lies outside the scope of this inquiry. The analysis is limited to structured examination and documentation.

At this point, both the dataset and the working configuration were still in flux. Small changes in file preparation or processing could shift the findings. Under such conditions, the observed patterns could reflect the behavior of the system as much as the images themselves. For that reason, conclusions about similarity or alignment were withheld.

Exploratory Testing With Interpretation Held Back

Exploration continued with steady attention to weak points in the pipeline. The analysis examined how sensitive the methods were to routine choices such as processing steps, crop boundaries, scaling, and feature representation. Different configurations were run side by side, and their outputs were compared across repeated runs to assess how stable they remained as conditions shifted.

A pattern emerged early. When controls remained loose, the findings could appear clean and persuasive even as the underlying conditions were still moving. Small changes could tighten clusters, widen gaps, or alter which images appeared closest. Such volatility can produce outputs that seem meaningful before the analysis has earned that level of confidence.

This stage served a practical purpose. It revealed which parts of the workflow held steady and which required tighter control.

Interpretation remained under restraint until the dataset, procedures, and constraints could be fixed in advance and rerun in the same way each time. Although qualifications were already in place for AI-generated outputs, it became clear that the broader direction of the inquiry also required careful control.

AI Collaboration

Statistical similarity as evidence: Deferred.

AI Output
High cosine similarity and low distance scores were reported as supporting evidence.

Author's Note
Statistical measures such as cosine similarity and distance scores were recorded carefully. High similarity was treated as numerical measurement only. Interpretive use of those scores was deferred until procedures and constraints were fully established.

By the close of this phase, several weaknesses had become clear. The dataset remained provisional and had yet to be fully defined. File naming and organization were inconsistent and lacked a standard structure. Findings sometimes shifted in ways that made clear the need for stronger constraint.

These difficulties required changes in the analysis. The source of the trouble lay in the organization and handling of the workflow. Correction was necessary before the analysis could proceed on a stable basis.

Emergence of Discipline

Once these weaknesses were recognized, the inquiry moved from exploration toward discipline. The next stage was devoted to defining clearer dataset boundaries, organizing files consistently, and establishing standard procedures.

The value of this phase lay in the lesson it made clear. Early coherence under flexible conditions carried risk. It showed how readily structure could appear before the analytical environment had stabilized.

From this point onward, the analysis proceeded more slowly and under stricter control. Progress came to be judged less by the volume of output than by the stability and transparency of the conditions under which that output was produced.

Entry 03

Entry 03

Book Reference: Chapter 3
Date: 16 February 2025
Phase: Visual Structural Alignment Testing

Section 1: Non-Separation in Feature Distributions

Objective:

To assess the structural alignment and visual correspondence between the Study Image crop and the Getty Image crop of *Les Barques, Régates à Argenteuil* (1874), and to determine whether any measurable divergence exists between the two images.

Approach:

A series of layer-overlay and pixel-level analysis methods were applied to evaluate structural and visual alignment. These included blending modes, alignment procedures, and histogram-based comparisons designed to test whether the images remain within the same visual feature space under multiple transformations.

Observation:

Across all applied methods, no significant divergence was observed. The Study and Getty crops consistently demonstrated structural congruence, tonal continuity, and pixel-level alignment.

Non-Separation Channels

Type	Script / Method	Nature of Non-Separation
Layer Overlay Alignment	Auto-Align Layers (Auto / Reposition)	Structural congruence observed between Study and Getty

Opacity Blending	50–60% transparency comparison	Visual compositional continuity between the images
Difference Blending Mode	Layer > Difference	Pixel-level overlap (black = high alignment) indicating structural similarity
Overlay / Soft Light Mode	Layer blending comparison	Tonal and color continuity confirmed
Luminosity Mode	Value-only comparison	Midtone and highlight structural consistency maintained
Layer Mask Selective Reveal	Mask + soft brush	Localized structural correspondence confirmed
Hue/Saturation Reduction	−50 to −70 saturation	Tonal alignment independent of color variations
Inversion Test	Ctrl + I	No material divergence observed upon inversion
Warp Grid Distortion Mapping	Edit > Transform > Warp	Geometric correspondence maintained
Guide/Ruler Measurement	Ruler tool / guides	Dock angle and horizon alignment consistent
Difference Map + Histogram	Histogram panel analysis	Pixel intensity overlap supports structural similarity
Edge Detection	Filter > Stylize > Find Edges	Contour similarity observed in brushstroke structure
Black & White Conversion	Structural abstraction	Form-based similarity persists
RGB Channel Histogram Comparison	Channel review (R/G/B)	Pigment distribution continuity confirmed
Curves Matching	Curves adjustment alignment	Tonal range equivalence maintained

Documented Outcomes

- Structural Congruence: High alignment observed across pixel-level and tonal comparisons
- Tonal and Color Continuity: Consistent compositional alignment across blending modes
- Brushstroke Direction and Pigment Distribution: Structural features and pigment behavior aligned across both images
- Divergence: No material divergence observed across any applied test

Section 2: Divergence in Feature Distributions

No Study/Getty/Monet versus non-Monet class-divergence testing was conducted or documented during this phase.

Summary of This Phase

• Early Stroke Differencing Exploration: Preliminary methods were explored but not fully implemented
• Successful Non-Separation Results: All applied tests confirmed structural and visual alignment between Study and Getty images

Conclusion

This phase demonstrated that the Study and Getty images of Les Barques, Régates à Argenteuil (1874) exhibit no measurable divergence in structural alignment, pigment distribution, or feature-level similarity. Under the applied methods, both images remain within the same visual feature space.

CHAPTER 4

Classical Image Analysis

After the exploratory phase, the inquiry turned toward tightening the environment in which the analysis was conducted. Earlier testing had revealed where the weaknesses lay. The next task was to bring greater order to the dataset and to the handling of the visual material itself.

This shift proceeded from a simple understanding: results merit trust only when data are handled consistently. The images served as the material of measurement. The way they were gathered, named, stored, and prepared would shape what could responsibly be said of them.

By this stage, the dataset drew upon material from many different sources. In the earlier phases, that mixture remained workable. As comparison became more exacting, those differences began to matter. The files varied in origin, resolution, cropping, color balance, and prior editing. Such variation could influence an outcome, and at times it was unclear whether a pattern arose from the image of the painting or from the treatment of the reproduction.

For that reason, the construction of the dataset became part of the analysis, with the understanding that further tightening would follow in later chapters. The material was brought into a shared working environment so that it could be accessed and handled uniformly. File naming was standardized, and handling rules were made consistent. The goal was straightforward: comparisons had to proceed under common conditions so that the findings would reflect the visual material itself.

Controlled Reference Crops

The testing also drew upon a small group of controlled digital crops taken from a well-documented Monet painting, *Les Barques, Régates à Argenteuil*, sourced through Getty Images. They provided a documented Monet reference that could be run alongside the Study Images, the broader Monet collection, and non-Monet comparisons, so that the behavior of the analysis might be observed across differing reference sets.

In later chapters, attention shifted from these Getty crops to the broader Monet reference collection. At that stage of the inquiry, the larger group served as the governing reference. Across those runs, *Les Barques, Régates à Argenteuil* repeatedly ranked closest to the Study Images, often appearing as the top match in the similarity outputs across differing test conditions. That proximity was recorded as an observed result of non-separation.

Initial Classical Analysis

Once the material was organized within a shared environment, the first round of structured classical analysis began. The testing methods focused on measurable properties, including texture, edges, frequency patterns, and broader color structure.

Texture and edge measurements showed irregular variation consistent with hand-applied paint. Frequency analysis revealed an absence of repeating or mechanical patterns. Color grouping and broader tonal comparison placed the Study Images in a similar region to the Monet references when all were handled under the same conditions. Broader structural measures likewise indicated a similar result.

When examined under identical conditions, the Getty-derived Monet crops appeared near both the Study Images and the established Monet material, while remaining distinct from non-Monet sources.

These findings were shaped in part by the way the dataset was assembled and prepared. Origin, resolution, and prior handling may still have influenced the outcome. For that reason, the stability observed in this phase applied only under those conditions. It established a point of reference while the question of alignment between the Study Images and the Monet references remained open.

Additional Controls Required

At this stage, several controls that later proved necessary still remained unfinished. Fixed cropping rules had yet to be applied consistently across image groups, so that each image could be examined under the same framing and portion of the surface. Duplicate files still required careful identification and removal, so that each image appeared only once even when present under different file names or sources. Further controls were needed to prevent overlap between comparison groups and to keep those groups properly balanced, so that no group would exert unintended influence on another. Feature representations still had to be recomputed under a single fixed model configuration, so that all numerical descriptions would arise under the same stable conditions. Distance evaluation across the full distribution remained to be carried out with calibrated error checks. Formal stress testing also lay ahead to assess how sensitive the findings were to resolution and to small differences in execution.

At the same time, a clearer understanding was emerging of the full range of elements that required constraint.

The outputs from this phase were used to determine what the dataset and the classical image methods could reasonably produce reliably under those conditions. The analysis showed which behaviors remained stable and where greater control would be required as the inquiry moved forward.

With that groundwork in place, attention turned from surface appearance toward deeper structural behavior within the images themselves.

Entry 04

Entry 04

Book Reference: Chapter 4
Date: 17 February 2025
Phase: Structural & Stylistic Similarity Testing

Section 1: Non-Separation in Feature Distributions

Objective:

To evaluate whether the Study and Getty crops of *Les Barques, Régates à Argenteuil* (1874) exhibit structural, stylistic, and feature-level continuity across computational analyses, and to assess whether they remain within the same visual feature space under multiple methods.

Approach:

A range of computational techniques was applied, including brushstroke analysis, pigment and spectral comparison, convolutional neural network (CNN) feature extraction, and dimensionality reduction methods. These procedures were used to examine structural alignment, brushstroke geometry, pigment distribution, and high-dimensional feature similarity.

Observation:

Across the applied methods, the Study and Getty images demonstrated consistent structural alignment, pigment continuity, and feature-space proximity. No measurable separation was observed under the tested conditions.

Non-Separation Channels

Type	Script / Method	Nature of Non-Separation
Brushstroke Angle	BrushAngle.py	Directional histogram

Mapping		overlap between Study and Getty
Brushstroke Similarity Metrics	SimilarityAnalysis.py	High cosine similarity (0.9808), low Chi-Square (0.0382), low EMD (0.0007)
Overlay + Difference Plot	HistoricalOverlay_DifferencePlot	Direct angular distribution overlap
Edge + Brushstroke Fusion	Edge_BrushAngle_Direction_Histograms_Comparison.py	Alignment of dominant stroke directions
Texture Depth Simulation	TextureDepthSimulation.py	Comparable impasto topology patterns
Impasto Depth Comparison	ImpastoDepthAnalysis.py	Similar gradient structures; variation interpreted as refinement
Paint Layer Transition Analysis	paint_layer_analysis.py	Shared structural layering behavior
Edge Detection Analysis	edge_detection.py	Comparable structural edge topology
Colorimetry & Spectral Matching	Colorimetry_Spectral_Matching.py	Shared dominant pigment distributions
Spectral Histogram Comparison	ColorimetrySpectralAnalysis.py	Similar RGB and spectral distributions
Spectral Deconvolution	AdvancedPigmentAnalysis.py	Consistent pigment clustering behavior
Pigment Aging Simulation	MonetPigmentAgingandComparison.py	Study remains within modeled pigment distribution
Spectral Similarity (EMD)	Reported values: 17.8705 → 5.9960	Moderate-to-strong palette proximity
CNN Brushstroke Classification	CNNBrushstrokeClassification	High classification confidence for Monet-style features

Fine-Tuned CNN (ResNet/VGG)	FurtherTraining.py	High classification consistency across test set
Feature Extraction (VGG16)	feature_extraction.py	High cosine similarity in feature space
PCA of Feature Space	PCAtSNE.py	Cluster proximity within feature manifold
t-SNE Embedding	PCAtSNE.py	Local neighborhood similarity in high-dimensional space
Unsupervised Stroke Clustering	K-Means + PCA	Shared cluster behavior in stroke distribution
AI-Based Stroke Differencing	AIBasedStrokeDifferencing	Consistent activation maps and stroke patterns

Documented Outcomes

• CNN Feature Extraction: Stable feature representations across Study and Getty images
• Cosine Similarity: High similarity observed between extracted feature vectors
• PCA & t-SNE: Study and Getty occupy close proximity within the feature manifold
• Color & Spectral Analysis: Consistent pigment distributions and tonal structure observed
• Structural Consistency: Brushstroke direction, impasto behavior, and edge topology aligned across analyses

Section 2: Divergence in Feature Distributions

Study/Getty/Monet versus non-Monet class-divergence testing was not conducted or documented during this phase.

Summary of This Phase

This phase focused on computational evaluation of structural and stylistic similarity between the Study and Getty images. Feature extraction, clustering, and dimensionality reduction methods indicated that both images occupy close proximity within the same feature space under the applied models.

Conclusion

Under the applied computational methods, the Study and Getty images of Les Barques, Régates à Argenteuil (1874) demonstrated no measurable separation in structural alignment, pigment behavior, or feature-space representation. The results indicate consistent similarity across multiple analytical approaches within the defined testing conditions.

CHAPTER 5

From Surface Impression to Structural Analysis

Once the basic measures of consistency were established, the inquiry moved from surface appearance toward structure. Surface qualities such as color harmony, atmosphere, brightness, and overall mood shape a first encounter with a painting. As noted earlier, these features are sensitive to lighting, reproduction, and display conditions, and therefore provide an unstable basis for comparison in digital analysis.

Structure provided a more stable basis. Here, structure refers to the arrangement of visual information within the image: the distribution of tones, the relation of forms to one another, and the way patterns recur or vary across space. These elements can be examined and measured under controlled conditions.

The question at this stage was straightforward: could structural features be extracted consistently across the Study Images, the Getty crops, the broader Monet reference group, and comparison material drawn from other artists, and then evaluated under the same conditions?

During this stage, artificial intelligence was used to assist in examining fine structural behavior, including brushstroke-level patterns, understood here as the physical mark of the brush: its direction, thickness, pressure, spacing, and overlap. Repeated across a surface, these small decisions form part of an artist's working method.

AI-Based Stroke Probing as Structural Diagnostics

Pretrained convolutional neural networks, computer systems designed to read and compare visual features such as edges, shapes, and textures, were applied as instruments of measurement. The purpose was to determine whether small-scale stroke patterns could be isolated in a stable and repeatable way under the conditions then in place. These constraints shaped what could be tested and how far the analysis could be carried within the limits of the available computing environment.

Execution remained stable throughout this stage. Findings were consistent across reruns, even when minor operational details shifted, including run order, session restarts, and routine file handling. Feature extraction likewise remained consistent across the Study Images, Getty crops, and reference material, converting visual data into numerical descriptions of edges, textures, and spatial patterns.

The available precision proved insufficient for isolating individual strokes or for separating image groups with consistency. The extracted features captured broad surface variation, yet lacked the refinement required to distinguish finer differences in brushwork across the available material.

Under the working conditions in place, brushstroke-level separation remained beyond reach. The tools, as configured, did not isolate that degree of detail in a dependable way. The limitations lay in the tools themselves, in the training of the models, in the precision with which strokes could be localized from the available reproductions, and in the practical limits of the computing environment.

Stroke-level analysis remained sensitive to resolution, stroke localization, sampling depth across the surface, and aspects of model design that favored broader texture over individual brush marks.

Heatmaps and cluster projections were used with measurable success at broader structural levels. These tools reduce complex visual information to condensed summaries, and the appearance of exactness can exceed what the testing conditions can support, particularly at finer levels such as individual brushstrokes. That success did not extend to brushstroke-level resolution. The outputs from this stage therefore required restraint in interpretation.

Later chapters move the inquiry into a more controlled environment and a broader reference base. This stage records what could responsibly be tested at that time and treats the stroke-probing outputs as observations bound to those conditions.

Methodological Realignment

By the close of this stage, the stroke-level effort had reached its practical limit under the conditions then in place. Further progress would have required supervised training with labeled examples, precise stroke segmentation to isolate individual marks, greater sampling depth across a wider surface area, and a more robust working environment. Those requirements lay beyond the available setup at that time.

The inquiry then turned away from the individual brushstroke and toward broader structural behavior that could be measured with greater consistency.

Entries 05 and 06

Entry 05

Book Reference: Chapter 5
Date: 18 February 2025
Phase: AI-Based Stroke Differencing

Section 1: Non-Separation in Feature Distributions

Objective:

To evaluate structural and feature-based similarity between the Study and Getty crops and a full-image Monet reference corpus, and to assess whether measurable proximity exists within a shared embedding framework.

Approach:

A Monet reference set of full painting images was introduced as a comparative baseline. Analysis was conducted using convolutional neural network (CNN) feature extraction, principal component analysis (PCA), and unsupervised clustering techniques. Additional methods included color histogram comparison, spectral analysis, and exploratory gradient-based heatmap generation.

Observation:

Feature extraction and dimensionality reduction methods executed successfully, producing stable numerical representations and enabling comparison across Study, Getty, and Monet images. However, clustering methods exhibited instability, and stroke-level differentiation was not reliably achieved under the applied conditions. Gradient-based visualization techniques failed due to architectural limitations.

Non-Separation Channels

Type	File / Script Examples	Nature of Non-Separation
CNN Feature Extraction (VGG16, pretrained)	AIBasedStrokeDifferencing.py	Feature vectors successfully generated (shape 25,088)
PCA Feature Space Visualization	PCA plots	High-dimensional features reduced for visual inspection
K-Means Unsupervised Clustering	KMeans over CNN features	Executed but unstable due to cluster collapse
Color Histogram Analysis	RGB histograms	Pigment distributions compared; pipeline stabilized
Spectral Curve Analysis (LAB)	LAB channel plots	Tonal differences evaluated independent of clustering
Gradient-Based Heatmap Attempt	Heatmap function	Failed due to absence of trained classifier head
Feature Normalization & NaN Handling	np.nan_to_num, dtype corrections	Numerical stability implemented post NaN propagation
Integrated Multi-Method Pipeline	Monet_Analysis.py	Combined feature extraction, PCA, clustering; instability persisted

Documented Outcomes

- CNN Feature Extraction: Stable high-dimensional feature representations were successfully generated
- PCA Dimensionality Reduction: Effective compression of feature space for comparative visualization
- Color & Spectral Analysis: Tonal and pigment distributions evaluated and stabilized after corrections

- Clustering Instability: K-Means clustering failed to produce reliable groupings due to NaN propagation and high-dimensional sensitivity
- Stroke-Level Limitations: Stroke-level clustering did not isolate consistent patterns under current methods
- Heatmap Limitations: Gradient-based methods were not applicable due to model architecture constraints
- Exploratory Classification: The stroke differencing approach remained diagnostic and exploratory rather than definitive

Section 2: Divergence in Feature Distributions

Study/Getty/Monet versus non-Monet class-divergence testing was not conducted or documented during this phase.

Summary of This Phase

This phase introduced AI-based stroke differencing as an exploratory diagnostic tool. While feature extraction and dimensionality reduction were successful, clustering instability and architectural limitations prevented reliable stroke-level differentiation. The phase established both the potential and the limitations of the approach.

Conclusion

This phase demonstrated that Study and Getty images can be evaluated within a shared feature-space framework alongside Monet reference images. While structural and feature-level similarity was observable under certain methods, instability in clustering and limitations in gradient-based analysis prevented definitive conclusions. The results are best understood as exploratory, establishing a foundation for refinement in subsequent phases.

Entry 06

Book Reference: Chapters 5
Date: 18 February 2025
Phase: Exploratory Manifold Testing

Section 1: Non-Separation in Feature Distributions

Objective:

To evaluate the feature-space proximity of the Study and Getty images relative to a Monet reference corpus, and to assess whether measurable alignment exists within a shared embedding framework.

Approach:

Feature extraction and dimensionality reduction techniques were applied, including convolutional neural network (CNN) feature extraction, principal component analysis (PCA), and color and spectral analysis. These methods were used to examine structural similarity and positional relationships within the feature manifold.

Observation:

Feature extraction and dimensionality reduction methods produced stable and consistent outputs, enabling comparative analysis across Study, Getty, and Monet images. The images occupied measurable regions within the shared feature space, with observable proximity under the applied methods. However, clustering-based methods remained unstable and did not produce reliable separations.

Non-Separation Channels

Type	Script / Artifact	Nature of Non-Separation
CNN Feature	AIBasedStrokeDiffer	Stable extraction of high-

Type	Script / Artifact	Nature of Non-Separation
Extraction (VGG16)	encing.py	dimensional feature vectors (25,088 dimensions)
PCA Feature Space Visualization	PCA plots	Dimensionality reduction executed; Study and Getty occupy measurable regions
Color Histogram Analysis	Integrated script	Pigment distribution comparison across datasets
Spectral Curve Analysis (LAB)	Integrated script	Tonal comparison independent of clustering
Multi-Technique Integrated Pipeline	Monet_Analysis.py	Combined feature extraction, PCA, and color analysis
Cluster Assignment (KMeans attempt)	AIBasedStrokeDifferencing.py	Attempted grouping; clustering instability observed
Feature Vector Validation	Console output	Dimensional consistency confirmed across all images

Documented Outcomes

Stable Components:

- CNN Feature Extraction: Consistent high-dimensional feature representations generated
- PCA Dimensionality Reduction: Feature-space relationships observable across datasets
- Color & Spectral Analysis: Shared tonal distributions observed under controlled conditions
- Feature Consistency: Dimensional stability maintained across Study, Getty, and Monet images

Limitations:

- KMeans Clustering: Failed to produce stable or interpretable clusters
- Clustering Instability: Collapse into dominant clusters prevented reliable separation
- Gradient-Based Methods: Heatmap generation not feasible due to model constraints
- Monet Pooling: Expansion of dataset did not resolve clustering instability

Section 2: Divergence in Feature Distributions

Objective:

To explore whether stroke-level or clustering-based methods could produce measurable separation between Monet and non-Monet feature distributions within a shared feature space.

Approach:

A non-Monet control set was introduced for exploratory divergence testing. Methods included conceptual CNN classification design, unsupervised clustering, and combined feature-based separation attempts.

Observation:

No stable or reliable separation between Monet and non-Monet works was achieved under the applied methods. Clustering approaches remained unstable, and classification-based methods were not implemented due to architectural limitations.

Separation Channels

Type	Script / Method	Documented Divergence
CNN Monet vs non-	Conceptual design	Not implemented

Type	Script / Method	Documented Divergence
Monet Classification Concept		
Combined CNN + Clustering	AIBasedStrokeDifferencing.py	No stable class boundary achieved
KMeans Stroke Clustering	Unsupervised clustering	Cluster collapse; weak separation
Monet Pooling Attempt	Dataset expansion	No improvement in separation
Gradient-Based Heatmap Attempt	Grad-CAM-like method	Failed due to model limitations

Documented Outcomes

- CNN Classification: Conceptual design only; no implemented classifier
- Combined Methods: No stable separation achieved using CNN + clustering
- Clustering Behavior: Collapse into dominant clusters prevented differentiation
- Dataset Expansion: Additional Monet images did not improve separation
- Heatmap Methods: Not viable under current architecture

Summary of This Phase

This phase evaluated Study and Getty images relative to a Monet reference corpus within a shared feature-space framework. While feature extraction and dimensionality reduction produced stable and interpretable outputs, clustering and divergence methods failed to generate reliable separation. These results indicated limitations in stroke-level and clustering-based approaches under the applied conditions.

Conclusion

This phase demonstrated that Study and Getty images can be consistently evaluated within a shared feature-space framework alongside Monet reference images. While structural and feature-level proximity was observable, attempts to differentiate Monet from non-Monet works were unsuccessful under the applied methods. These limitations informed a methodological shift toward more stable manifold-based approaches in subsequent phases.

CHAPTER 6

Stability Under Partial Control

In this chapter, the analysis turned more fully toward broader structural measures, drawing upon feature extraction, similarity with distance scoring, and projection tools. A simple two-group classifier was added as a further check, and autoencoder reconstruction was introduced to observe how works were rebuilt under a model trained on Monet references. These testing methods addressed larger structure rather than the individual brushstroke and were rerun under the same settings with fewer sources of variation.

The analysis at this stage depended on stable conditions: consistent processing, controlled resolution, and sufficient sampling across the image surface. Small differences in cropping, scaling, or in the computing environment itself could still alter the outcome.

The broader structural tools used here depended less on such variability. They operated through more general features that held steadier within the same pipeline, so that reruns were less prone to drift.

The central question at this stage was one of repeatability. When visual inputs passed through a fixed pipeline under fixed settings, did the outputs return in the same form each time?

What Stayed Steady Across Repeated Runs

Across repeated runs at this stage, feature extraction consistently converted each work into a numerical description of its visual structure. When inputs were processed under fixed conditions, these descriptions showed very little variation. Several tools were then used to compare the resulting measurements.

Cosine Similarity and Distance Scores

Cosine similarity is one means of measuring closeness in feature space, the numerical domain created when images are translated into measurements. In these runs, cosine similarity and distance scores repeatedly placed the Study Images and the Getty crops near one another, with similar spacing relative to the Monet reference set. These relationships remained stable across repeated runs.

Principal Component Analysis

PCA compresses many measurements into a two-dimensional plot so that patterns can be seen more readily. At this stage, it produced much the same layout across runs. The amount of variation from the original data shown in that plot remained about the same.

t-Distributed Stochastic Neighbor Embedding

t-SNE was used to place images on a two-dimensional plot according to similarity. At this stage, it did not produce clearly separated groups. The sample size remained fixed, and the feature measurements overlapped too substantially for distinct clusters to emerge. That mixed pattern persisted across reruns.

Classifier Testing

A binary classifier was also tested. The model was trained using images grouped as Monet and non-Monet. It used measurements drawn from the images to learn a boundary between them and then placed new images on one side or the other.

It performed well on the images used for training. That performance declined when the model was tested on new inputs. This indicated that the separation between the two groups did not carry forward cleanly beyond the training set.

Taken together, the findings at this stage showed repeatability in the outputs, while separation between groups remained inconsistent.

Autoencoder-Based Reconstruction

This stage also introduced autoencoder reconstruction. The model was trained to compress an image and then rebuild it from that compressed form. When trained on Monet images, it learned the visual patterns common within that set. If a new image matched those patterns, the rebuilt version looked very similar and the difference was small. If it did not match, the rebuilt version lost more detail and the difference was larger. In this way, the model indicated that one image was more similar to the training set than another under that configuration.

Under the setup used at this stage, Monet works reconstructed with low error values within a relatively narrow range. The Getty crop and the Study Image also fell within that range. Selected non-Monet works produced higher reconstruction error under the same model.

Taken together, these results indicated that the Study Image and the Getty crop aligned more closely with the reconstruction behavior of the Monet reference works than with the non-Monet material under this configuration.

That observation still required restraint. It remained bound to the dataset and to the level of control reached at that stage.

Why Stability Can Be a Risk

Repeatable results can be encouraging. They can also mislead. When the same analysis is run repeatedly, the procedure may settle into a steady pattern. At times that steadiness reflects genuine structure present in the images. At other times it reflects the constraints of the pipeline or routine choices in how the process is carried out.

For that reason, stability itself became an object of testing. The inquiry had to determine whether stable outputs were genuinely earned or instead arose as a byproduct of partial control.

Artificial intelligence systems learn from the data and conditions provided to them. When the same inputs and settings are used repeatedly, the outputs can assume an appearance of steadiness. That appearance required careful management, especially while the pipeline still permitted forms of variation that had yet to be fully defined.

AI Collaboration
Stability interpretation: Bounded.

AI Output
Observed patterns appeared stable across repeated tests.

Author's Note

Stable results required close examination of the conditions producing them before any weight could be assigned.

Moving Beyond Simple Repetition

To determine whether the apparent stability reflected the images themselves or the pipeline surrounding them, the inquiry moved beyond simple reruns. Parts of the process were deliberately altered. Image size, normalization steps, similarity measures, and dimensionality settings were changed to see whether the patterns would persist.

The purpose was straightforward. If the patterns held under those changes, that would point toward deeper structural behavior. If they shifted readily, that would point back to the pipeline as the principal cause.

Stability Without Separation

Stability without strong separation persisted across feature extraction, similarity measurement, dimensionality reduction, and reconstruction testing. When settings were adjusted, the broader patterns remained largely intact.

By the close of this stage, the behavior of the tools under partial control was better understood. Stable-looking results could appear before the process had been fully tightened.

Stability alone carried little value while the environment still allowed variation. Apparent differences arising under particular settings likewise carried limited value until those settings had been understood and vetted.

What Had to Happen Next

Before repeated results could be relied upon, the conditions producing them had to be made more controlled. That meant tightening the selection and preparation of images, standardizing processing steps, checking for duplicates, fixing model settings, and reducing the room for unintended variation.

It also meant strengthening the computing environment. Some of the next steps required more memory, greater GPU capacity, and a more stable execution pipeline, so that larger runs and stricter controls could be carried out without compromise in image size, sampling depth, or model choice. In the same way, before differences between groups could be used to draw conclusions, the testing setup needed to be made more controlled. Dataset structure, training images, evaluation procedures, and measurement methods all required review and tightening.

The next chapter serves as a transition. It records a concentrated period of methodological improvement, directed toward tighter control, a stronger working environment, and fewer sources of variation. It closes with a brief round of testing that confirms the improved setup runs cleanly before the inquiry moves forward.

Entries 07-08

Entry 07

Book Reference: Chapter 6
Date: 22 February 2025
Phase: Feature-Space & Binary Classifier Testing

Section 1: Non-Separation in Feature Distributions

Objective:

To quantify the feature-space proximity between Study, Getty, and Monet images, and to assess whether the Study and Getty images occupy similar regions within a shared feature manifold.

Approach:

CNN-based feature extraction, cosine similarity analysis, and dimensionality reduction techniques (PCA and t-SNE) were applied. These methods were used to evaluate structural and stylistic similarity within a common feature-space representation.

Observation:

Feature extraction and dimensionality reduction methods produced stable outputs, enabling quantitative comparison across Study, Getty, and Monet images. Measurable proximity was observed within the feature space under the applied methods.

Non-Separation Channels

Type	Script / Artifact	Nature of Non-Separation
CNN Feature Extraction (VGG16, pretrained)	VGG16FeatureExtraction.py	Generated feature vectors representing texture, edge structure, and composition
Cosine Similarity Matrix	compute_cosine_similarity()	Getty–Study cosine similarity ≈ 0.62, indicating

Type	Script / Artifact	Nature of Non-Separation
		feature-space alignment
PCA Dimensionality Reduction	apply_pca_tsne()	Reduced dimensionality; ~69% variance explained by first components
t-SNE Visualization	apply_pca_tsne()	Local proximity patterns observed (limited by sample size)
Image Preprocessing & Standardization	Resizing & cropping pipeline	Ensured consistent input structure
Feature-Space Baseline	NumPy feature vectors	Enabled comparison independent of classification boundaries

Documented Outcomes

- CNN Feature Extraction: Stable feature representations generated across datasets
- Cosine Similarity: Measurable similarity observed between Study and Getty
- PCA & t-SNE: Feature-space relationships visualized and evaluated
- Feature-Space Relationships: Proximity observed under applied methods

Section 2: Divergence in Feature Distributions

Objective:

To assess whether Monet and non-Monet works can be separated within the feature space, and to evaluate whether Study and Getty exhibit measurable divergence from non-Monet reference images.

Approach:

A binary CNN classifier (fine-tuned VGG16) was implemented to distinguish Monet (positive class) from non-Monet works (negative class). Training, validation, and test performance were evaluated using a folder-based class labeling system.

Observation:

While training and validation performance indicated partial learning, the model failed to generalize to unseen data. No reliable separation between Monet and non-Monet works was achieved under the applied conditions.

Separation Channels

Type	Script / Method	Documented Divergence
Binary CNN Classifier	Fine-tuned VGG16	Implemented Monet vs non-Monet classification
Training Performance	10 epochs	Training accuracy reached 1.0
Validation Performance	Evaluation set	~83.33% accuracy
Test Evaluation	Held-out data	Test accuracy = 0.0; failure to generalize
Data Labeling	Folder structure	Class labels defined by directory organization

Documented Outcomes

- Binary CNN Classifier: Model trained successfully but did not generalize
- Training Performance: High accuracy achieved during training
- Validation Performance: Partial generalization observed
- Test Performance: Failure to generalize to unseen data

- Classification Limitation: Model unable to reliably separate Monet and non-Monet works

Summary of This Phase

This phase confirmed that feature-space similarity between Study, Getty, and Monet images can be quantified using extraction and dimensionality reduction methods. However, classification-based divergence testing proved unreliable, with models failing to generalize beyond training data. These results reinforced the limitations of classification-based approaches under the applied conditions.

Conclusion

This phase demonstrated that Study and Getty images exhibit measurable proximity to Monet images within a shared feature-space framework. However, attempts to separate Monet and non-Monet works using classification methods were unsuccessful due to generalization failure. These findings further supported a shift away from classification-based approaches toward more stable manifold-based methods in subsequent phases.

Entry 08

Book Reference: Chapter 6
Date: 22 February 2025
Phase: Autoencoder Reconstruction Testing

Section 1: Non-Separation in Feature Distributions

Objective:

To evaluate the feature-space alignment of the Study and Getty images relative to a Monet-trained representation, using reconstruction error as a quantitative measure of similarity under a shared model.

Approach:

A convolutional autoencoder was trained on Monet reference images to learn color, tonal transitions, and structural patterns. Study and Getty images were then passed through the trained model, and reconstruction error (mean squared error, MSE) was measured and compared against the Monet baseline range.

Observation:

Both Study and Getty images produced reconstruction errors within the range observed for Monet reference images under the trained model. This indicates that, under the applied representation, both images are consistent with the learned feature distribution.

Non-Separation Channels

Type	Script / Artifact	Nature of Non-Separation
Monet Autoencoder Training	TrainAutoencoder.py	Learned Monet-specific color and tonal structure
Training Loss	training_loss.png	Stable loss decrease (~0.052

Type	Script / Artifact	Nature of Non-Separation
Convergence		→ ~0.014)
Monet Reconstruction Validation	reconstructions.png	Monet images reconstructed with preserved structure
Reconstruction Error Framework	InferReconstructionError.py	MSE used as similarity metric
Getty Reconstruction Baseline	Getty_reconstruction.png	MSE = 0.00604
Study Reconstruction Evaluation	Study_reconstruction.png	MSE = 0.00775
Comparative MSE Analysis	Summary metrics	Study and Getty fall within Monet baseline range (~0.006–0.008)

Documented Outcomes

- Getty Reconstruction: Low reconstruction error observed (MSE = 0.00604)
- Study Reconstruction: Low reconstruction error observed (MSE = 0.00775)
- Monet Baseline Range: Reconstruction error for Monet images observed in the range ~0.006–0.008
- Consistency: Study and Getty reconstruction errors fall within the Monet baseline range under the trained model
- Internal Behavior: No measurable separation observed between Study, Getty, and Monet under reconstruction conditions

Section 2: Divergence in Feature Distributions

Objective:

To assess whether non-Monet works exhibit measurable divergence from the Monet-trained representation, using reconstruction error as a comparative signal.

Approach:

A non-Monet reference set (including Van Gogh, Cézanne, Picasso, and Matisse) was evaluated using the same trained autoencoder. Reconstruction error values were compared against the Monet baseline range to assess divergence behavior.

Observation:

non-Monet works produced consistently higher reconstruction error values than Monet, Study, and Getty images under the trained model. This indicates measurable divergence from the learned representation.

Separation Channels

Type	Script / Artifact	Documented Divergence
Van Gogh Reconstruction	vangogh1_reconstruction.png	MSE = 0.01443
Cézanne Reconstruction	cezanne1_reconstruction.png	MSE = 0.01518
Picasso Reconstruction	pablo1_reconstruction.png	MSE = 0.01835
Matisse Reconstruction	matisse1_reconstruction.png	MSE = 0.02957
Error Band Comparison	Summary metrics	Monet: ~0.006–0.008 vs non-Monet: ~0.014–0.03

Documented Outcomes

- Reconstruction Error Separation: non-Monet works produced higher error values than Monet baseline
- Error Band Distinction: Clear numerical separation observed between Monet and non-Monet ranges
- Pattern Behavior: Reconstruction error increased with stylistic distance under the trained model

- Relative Positioning: Study remains within the Monet baseline range under reconstruction conditions

Summary of This Phase

This phase applied autoencoder-based reconstruction as a quantitative method for evaluating feature-space similarity. Study and Getty images produced reconstruction errors within the Monet baseline range, while non-Monet works exhibited consistently higher error values. The results indicate that reconstruction error can function as a comparative signal under the trained representation, while remaining dependent on model structure and dataset composition.

Conclusion

Under the trained autoencoder model, Study and Getty images produced reconstruction behavior consistent with Monet reference images, while non-Monet works exhibited measurable divergence. These results demonstrate the utility of reconstruction error as a comparative signal within a learned feature representation, while remaining conditional on model design and training data. Further refinement is required to assess the robustness and generalizability of this approach.

Part II

Transitional Hardening and Safeguard Constraints

CHAPTER 7

Transitional Interval:
A Period of Restart and Methodical Control

Orientation to the Interval

This chapter gathers a long stretch of work into a single concentrated interval. Its purpose was to bring the process, in its entirety, under stricter control.

By this point, certain results had begun to recur. Patterns appeared stable. The Study Images consistently appeared near Monet references. That proximity seemed promising and helped sustain the work. Yet it had emerged before the analytical environment had been fully brought under control. Under conditions that remain only partly hardened, repeated structure carries only limited weight.

The observed stability may have reflected structure within the material itself. It may equally have reflected the manner in which the workflow had been arranged. The responsible course was therefore to pause the search for further answers, examine the foundation, and tighten control.

This interval was defined by restraint and by the deliberate closing of pathways through which error might enter. The purpose was to ensure that whatever testing followed would rest upon more stable conditions.

Earlier outputs were archived, and the analytical workflows that had produced them were documented. This was done to better control the conditions that produced the results before continuing the analysis.

Stabilizing the Environment

During this interval, attention shifted to the environment in which testing would occur. GPU behavior and numerical computation can vary. Software can change even when code remains untouched. Updates can proceed silently in the background. Libraries and drivers can shift in version. Default settings can change. Certain steps can behave differently after a restart or reinstall. Taken separately, such changes may appear minor. Across many runs, however, they can accumulate and gradually alter the results. Where control is loose, results can drift.

Several measures were therefore taken. Software versions were fixed so that unintended updates could not enter the process. Automatic updating was restricted, ensuring that untracked changes would exert no influence on the analysis. File paths and naming conventions were standardized so that undocumented choices would not enter the workflow through disorder. Hardware consistency was treated as a priority so that the computational setup would perform predictably over time. Network access was restricted so that external services, cloud processes, or background downloads would have no effect on execution; all computation was required to proceed locally under controlled conditions. Background processes were minimized, reducing the likelihood that unrelated system activity would consume resources, alter timing, or introduce variation between runs.

At this stage, the system had to remain idle without change: stable, predictable, and unchanged over time.

Making the System Restartable

The next task was to ensure that the system could be shut down, restarted, and still return the same outputs under the same conditions. Each result had to stand on its own, without dependence on uptime, prior execution, or residual temporary data.

Execution scripts were written in a fixed and explicit order so that each step followed the same sequence every time. Cached results were cleared between runs, preventing earlier outputs from influencing later ones. Temporary files were removed.

Certain parts of machine learning depend on randomness. If that randomness is not controlled, identical tests can produce different results from one run to the next. Small variations can enter through random starting values, data ordering, or internal sampling steps within the model. Taken individually, these differences may appear minor. Across repeated runs, however, they can introduce inconsistency into the outputs.

To prevent this, sources of randomness were fixed so that each run began from the same point and followed the same path. Under those conditions, any remaining differences could be traced to the data or to the procedure itself. The result was that repeated outputs reflected the defined procedure alone, with leftover data, hidden memory, and background activity kept outside the result.

Dataset Hardening

Earlier phases had revealed possible weaknesses in the selection and organization of the visual material. This stage addressed those weaknesses by tightening the rules of inclusion and enforcing clearer separation between groups. The concern was straightforward. Overlap can enter through shared files, duplicate material, or uneven handling, and this can make two groups appear closer than they are.

A uniform cropping policy was applied across all material so that each image was framed according to the same rules. Duplicate and near-duplicate reproductions were removed. Exact copies and highly similar versions of the same image were identified and excluded, preventing similarity scores from being strengthened by repetition. non-Monet images were clearly grouped and kept separate, reducing the chance that stylistic resemblance or shared catalog sources would blur distinctions. The dataset was also checked to make sure no identifying information was leaking into the analysis. File organization and labeling were examined to ensure that information about identity could not exert unintended influence on model behavior.

These measures removed pathways through which similarity might be strengthened by the structure of the dataset itself.

Rebuilding Embeddings From Scratch

At this point in the transition, testing was opened again, though under tighter discipline. All earlier embeddings, the numerical representations generated in prior phases, were set-aside so that earlier assumptions and processing choices would not carry forward into the hardened pipeline. Embeddings were rebuilt from the beginning under the revised rules, using the same procedure across the full set.

Throughout this interval, artificial intelligence played a supporting role in tracking and summarizing prior steps, flagging inconsistencies, and assisting in organizing procedural flow. When AI-generated language suggested alignment or emerging trends, that language was treated as bound to the specific conditions that had produced it.

AI Collaboration
Framing without a defined Monet class: Unsupported.

AI Output
Generated interpretive language suggesting Monet alignment.

Author's Note
Interpretive language was set-aside when it went beyond what the embedding data supported.

New embeddings were then computed from the beginning using frozen, self-supervised models. Here, "frozen" means that the model's internal weights remained fixed and were never updated during testing. A self-supervised model is one that had previously learned general visual structure from large image collections without being trained to recognize particular artists.

Each image was processed using one model and consistent settings every time. Measurements were taken under a stable setup, with no changes to the model during testing.

Image size was treated as a test condition in its own right. The material was analyzed at one fixed resolution, then resized and analyzed again from the beginning at a higher resolution. Each run stood independently. Measurements from differing resolutions were kept separate.

The results stayed consistent even when image size was changed and the analysis was run again from the beginning. This showed that the process remained stable.

Distance Measured Across Full Distributions

Earlier testing had often focused on individual pairings, asking how close one image stood to another. During this interval, that approach was expanded. Distance was evaluated across entire groups so that the position of each image could be understood within the larger structure of the dataset rather than in isolation. This made it possible to see whether a pattern held across many relationships instead of appearing only in a few pairings.

In general terms, more than one way of calculating distance in feature space was used. Multiple distance measures were applied, each defining closeness somewhat differently. Some compared how similar the patterns were, some measured how different they were overall, and others looked at how values were spread across the group.

Separately, a visual comparison was run to see which parts of the images the model focused on most. The Getty image and the Study Image showed nearly identical focus, with a similarity score of about 0.98 in that run.

During this phase, the heatmaps were not judged by how they looked. Instead, they were turned into numbers that could be compared. The focus was on how consistent the attention was under controlled conditions, rather than taking the heatmaps as proof of what the model was seeing.

The questions were practical. Was the attention pattern stable when the same image was run again, that is, did it highlight the same regions each time under identical settings? Did the attention shift in any meaningful way when neither the image nor the processing steps had changed? Did attention patterns produce clear and repeatable differences between Study, Getty, and Monet material, or did they continue to overlap without forming distinct groups?

Under controlled conditions, the model focused on the same areas each time. That consistency did not show clear separation and instead suggested overlap between the Study, Getty, and Monet images.

Signature-Region Isolation

The Study Image includes a signature that reads "Claude Monet." Signatures are small but noticeable, and the model can sometimes pay too much attention to them, causing a small area of the image to affect the overall result more than it should.

To minimize this risk, signature regions were isolated and measured separately from the full images. Grad-CAM attention mapping was used to check how the model focused on the signature areas in both the Getty and Study Images. The Getty signature, as the confirmed Monet reference, was used for comparison. The test examined whether the Study signature produced a similar attention pattern to the Getty signature and whether the results remained consistent.

Signature areas were cropped to the same size and position, and brightness and contrast were normalized to minimize differences from lighting, photography, or scanning.

Tests were repeated with consistent settings, confirming that identical inputs returned identical outputs.

The result was as expected: the Study and Getty signatures produced similar attention patterns. This was due to their shared visual features. As designed, the test would likely succeed and expected to show that the attention patterns were consistent. This was not a failure-prone test. It was about confirming the stability of the model's attention patterns, which is why the outcome was predictable and intended.

Autoencoder Stress Testing

For stress testing, the Monet-trained autoencoder was evaluated within the hardened pipeline. The model compresses an image and rebuilds it based on patterns learned from Monet training material. Reconstruction error measures the difference between the original image and the rebuilt version. Lower error indicates a closer match to the learned patterns, while higher error shows weaker correspondence.

Reconstruction error remained stable across repeated runs. Monet images reconstructed with low error values, while selected non-Monet images had higher error values. The Study Image fell within the range adjacent to Monet works under this model.

This ranking showed how the model behaved under consistent conditions, reflecting how it responded to the material based on what it had learned. Stable reconstruction, in this case, means the model behaved predictably during the tests.

The Function of the Transitional Chapter

During this phase, results sometimes appeared inconsistent from one round of testing to the next. At times, the Study Images seemed to align closely with the Monet references, while at other times the connection appeared weaker, or the boundary between Monet and non-Monet images became less clear. These fluctuations pointed to issues with the testing environment. The dataset was still being refined, inclusion rules were still being enforced, and parts of the processing and evaluation pipeline were still being adjusted. Under such conditions, even small differences in what entered the dataset, how it was processed, or how it was normalized could shift the results, leading to changes in image grouping

Because of this, inconsistency was treated as a signal that the setup still had room for improvement. It showed that uneven image quality, duplicate or nearly duplicate material, mixed resolutions, varying crops, and other differences in handling could either strengthen or weaken the similarity between images. Until these issues were addressed, any findings, indicating separation or lack of separation, had to be seen as influenced by an incomplete dataset and workflow.

This chapter records the work done to address these issues and ensure that later testing would be reliable. Future findings, whether supporting separation or non-separation, would rest on a system that had been thoroughly checked, refined, and stabilized. From this point forward, any instability or inconsistency would be minimized, ensuring that the results were grounded in a controlled framework.

Entries 09-18

Entry 09

Book Reference: Chapter 7
Date: 23 February 2025
Phase: System Configuration & Image Infrastructure

Objective:

To establish the system configuration, image acquisition workflow, and computational infrastructure required for subsequent analytical testing.

Procedures Completed:

This phase focused on system setup, image capture workflow development, and technical preparation in advance of analytical testing. Hardware was configured and system architecture established to support future computational requirements.

Image acquisition procedures were developed and tested to ensure standardized input for later analysis. In parallel, the computational pipeline was prepared, including initial preprocessing structures and workflow design to support downstream analytical processes.

Infrastructure was developed to support data handling, processing, and execution of future testing phases.

Focus Areas:

- System Configuration and Hardware Setup: Configuration of hardware and system architecture
- Image Acquisition Workflow Preparation: Development of standardized image capture procedures
- Technical Pipeline Preparation: Preparation of preprocessing and computational workflows

- Infrastructure Development: Establishment of systems to support analytical execution

Testing Conducted:

No formal analytical testing or comparative modeling was conducted during this phase. All work was preparatory in nature.

Artifacts Produced:

- System Configuration Documentation: Records of system setup and configuration
- Image Capture Workflow Notes: Documentation of acquisition procedures
- Pipeline Preparation Scripts: Supporting scripts for computational workflow preparation

Status:

This phase concluded with system infrastructure and workflows established to support subsequent analytical testing. No testing results were generated during this phase.

Entry 10

Book Reference: Chapter 7
Date: 28 February 2025
Phase: Model Optimization & Planning

Objective:

To optimize model architecture and prepare system infrastructure for subsequent analytical testing, ensuring robustness and scalability of the computational framework.

Procedures Completed:

This phase focused on model refinement, architectural adjustments, and system planning. Efforts were directed toward improving reconstruction quality, enhancing feature representation, and preparing the computational environment for future testing.

Model performance issues, including reconstruction blur, were diagnosed and addressed through architectural and training modifications. Input resolution was increased to improve output fidelity, and the dimensionality of the bottleneck layer was expanded to support richer feature encoding.

The network architecture was further refined by increasing depth and width, and by transitioning to a U-Net structure with skip connections to preserve spatial information during encoding and decoding. Training duration was extended to allow improved convergence, and hyperparameters were adjusted to optimize performance.

The Monet dataset was expanded to improve model generalization and support more stable training behavior.

System Planning:

- Workstation Specification Planning: Defined hardware requirements, including GPU (RTX 4090), memory, and CPU configuration
- Linux Operating System Evaluation: Assessed Linux-based environments for improved computational performance
- Hardware Expansion Planning: Prepared for scaling to support larger datasets and increased computational demand

Conceptual Next Steps (Not Executed):

- Batch Processing Design: Planned scalable workflows for large image datasets
- Alternative Error Metrics: Considered SSIM and MAE for future evaluation
- Threshold-Based Classification Concept: Proposed classification framework based on output thresholds

Testing Conducted:

No finalized analytical testing or comparative modeling was conducted during this phase. Activities remained focused on optimization, configuration, and preparation.

Artifacts Produced:

- Model Revision Notes: Documentation of architectural and configuration changes
- Architecture Modification Drafts: Records of network design updates, including U-Net transition
- System Planning Documentation: Hardware and infrastructure planning records

Status:

This phase concluded with model architecture and system infrastructure refined and prepared for subsequent analytical testing cycles.

Entry 11

Book Reference: Chapter 7
Date: 9 March 2025
Phase: Hardware Evaluation & Acquisition

Objective:

To evaluate hardware suitability and validate infrastructure requirements necessary to support deep learning workflows prior to system acquisition.

Procedures Completed:

This phase focused on assessing hardware capabilities and validating system readiness for high-resolution image processing and deep learning tasks. No stylistic or comparative analysis was performed.

System components were evaluated to ensure they met the computational demands required for model training, preprocessing, and data handling. The review included GPU performance, CPU threading capacity, memory sufficiency, storage throughput, and system stability under expected workloads.

System Evaluation and Purchase Review:

- Aurora R16 Hardware Assessment: Evaluated overall system suitability for deep learning workloads
- GPU Capability (RTX 4090): Assessed performance for high-resolution image processing and model training
- CPU Threading Capacity: Verified ability to support parallel preprocessing tasks

- RAM Sufficiency: Confirmed capacity for handling large image datasets
- NVMe Storage Throughput: Evaluated read/write performance for data-intensive operations
- PSU and Thermal Stability: Verified power headroom and thermal performance under load
- Operating System Flexibility: Assessed compatibility with Linux and WSL environments
- Expansion Constraints: Reviewed scalability within a single-GPU configuration

Testing Conducted:

No analytical or comparative image testing was conducted during this phase. Activities were limited to infrastructure validation and hardware readiness assessment.

Artifacts Produced:

- Hardware Evaluation Notes: Documentation of system capability and performance considerations
- System Specification Review Documentation: Records of hardware specifications and validation outcomes

Status:

This phase concluded with infrastructure requirements validated and hardware suitability confirmed for deep learning workflows. It served as a preparatory step prior to system acquisition and subsequent testing phases.

Entry 12

Book Reference: Chapter 7
Date: 18 March 2025
Phase: Linux Environment Setup

Objective:

To install and configure a Linux-based operating system and prepare the Aurora R16 workstation environment for deep learning frameworks and future AI workloads.

Procedures Completed:

This phase focused on operating system installation, system configuration, and environment preparation. No stylistic or comparative image analysis was conducted.

A Linux distribution was installed on the Aurora R16 workstation, with disk partitioning and boot configuration managed to ensure system stability and performance. Driver installation was completed with emphasis on GPU compatibility, including setup and verification of NVIDIA drivers and the CUDA toolkit to support GPU-accelerated computation.

Networking was configured to ensure stable connectivity for system updates, framework installation, and external dependencies. System repositories were established and updated to maintain compatibility and security.

System Readiness Under Linux:

- Hardware Recognition: Verified detection of RTX 4090 GPU, CPU, RAM, and storage devices
- CUDA and Driver Validation: Confirmed CUDA toolkit and NVIDIA drivers are properly installed

- Environment Preparation: Prepared system for installation of deep learning frameworks (e.g., TensorFlow, PyTorch)
- Compatibility Verification: Ensured system configuration supports anticipated AI workloads

Testing Conducted:

No analytical image testing or comparative modeling was conducted during this phase. Activities were limited to operating system installation and infrastructure preparation.

Artifacts Produced:

- Linux Installation Notes: Documentation of installation and configuration steps
- Driver Configuration Documentation: Records of NVIDIA driver and CUDA setup
- CUDA Readiness Verification: Confirmation of GPU-accelerated environment readiness

Status:

This phase concluded with the system fully configured under Linux and prepared to support deep learning frameworks and subsequent analytical workflows.

Entry 13

Book Reference: Chapter 7
Date: 19 March 2025
Phase: Controlled Internet Access Planning

Objective:

To configure network security and establish controlled outbound internet access for future tasks, including image acquisition and automated data collection.

Procedures Completed:

This phase focused on firewall configuration, outbound traffic control, and planning for restricted network access. No analytical image testing or modeling was conducted.

A firewall was configured using UFW (Uncomplicated Firewall) to manage network traffic and enforce security policies. Default outbound deny rules were implemented to restrict all external communication unless explicitly permitted. Outbound traffic rules were reviewed and refined to allow only authorized services.

Network activity was monitored using tools such as *iftop* to validate rule enforcement and ensure compliance with defined traffic policies.

Outgoing Traffic Control Setup:

- UFW Configuration: Installed and configured firewall rules for traffic management
- Default Outbound Deny: Enforced restricted outbound communication by default
- Rule Management: Reviewed and adjusted rules for controlled external access

- Connection Monitoring: Verified active connections and traffic behavior

Network Restriction Strategy:

- Controlled Web Access: Enabled internet access only when required
- Port Management: Temporarily allowed HTTP/HTTPS (ports 80/443) as needed
- DNS Configuration: Ensured proper resolution while restricting unauthorized access
- Lockdown Considerations: Evaluated stricter outbound control configurations

Image Scraping Planning:

- Controlled Access Design: Planned restricted network usage for scraping workflows
- Permission Management: Defined access controls for automated data retrieval processes

Testing Conducted:

No analytical image testing or comparative modeling was conducted during this phase. Activities were limited to network configuration and controlled access planning.

Artifacts Produced:

- Firewall Configuration Notes: Documentation of UFW setup and rule definitions
- Network Rule Documentation: Records of outbound traffic policies and configurations

- Scraping Workflow Planning Documentation: Plans for controlled network access during data acquisition

Status:

This phase concluded with network security configuration and controlled access policies established, enabling secure and restricted internet usage for subsequent data acquisition tasks.

Entry 14

Book Reference: Chapter 7
Date: 20 March 2025
Phase: Controlled Outbound Access

Objective:

To implement and validate controlled outbound network access under Linux, ensuring secure communication and restricted internet usage for future data acquisition tasks.

Procedures Completed:

This phase focused on refining firewall configuration and validating outbound traffic control behavior under restrictive policies. No analytical image testing or comparative modeling was conducted.

Firewall rules were configured using UFW (Uncomplicated Firewall), with default outbound deny policies enforced to restrict all external communication unless explicitly permitted. Existing rules were reviewed and adjusted to ensure that only authorized connections were allowed.

Additional evaluation was conducted to observe how active connections behaved under restrictive policies, ensuring that enforcement mechanisms functioned as intended. Network activity was monitored using tools such as *iftop* to verify real-time traffic behavior and compliance with defined rules.

Outgoing Traffic Control Setup:

- UFW Configuration: Established firewall rules for outbound traffic control
- Default Outbound Deny: Enforced restricted communication by default

- Rule Review and Adjustment: Validated authorized connection pathways
- Connection Behavior Evaluation: Assessed system behavior under restrictive policies
- Traffic Monitoring: Verified network activity using real-time monitoring tools

Network Restriction Strategy:

- Controlled Web Access: Limited external connectivity to required use cases
- Port Management: Temporarily enabled or disabled HTTP/HTTPS ports (80/443) as needed
- DNS Configuration: Ensured controlled resolution while restricting unauthorized endpoints
- Lockdown Evaluation: Explored stricter outbound control configurations

Image Scraping Planning:

- Controlled Access Design: Defined restricted network usage for scraping workflows
- Permission Management: Established access control strategies for automated downloads

Testing Conducted:

No analytical image testing or comparative modeling was conducted during this phase. Activities were limited to validation of firewall configuration and outbound access control behavior.

Artifacts Produced:

- Firewall Configuration Notes: Documentation of UFW rules and policy enforcement
- Network Rule Documentation: Records of outbound traffic configurations
- Controlled Scraping Workflow Plans: Documentation of access strategies for secure data acquisition

Status:

This phase concluded with outbound traffic control validated and network behavior confirmed under restrictive policies, supporting secure and controlled access for future data acquisition tasks.

Entry 15

Book Reference: Chapter 7
Date: 30 March 2025
Phase: Workflow Structuring

Objective:

To organize prior project outputs, define the next steps in the analytical workflow, and structure upcoming testing phases to ensure continuity across all stages of analysis.

Procedures Completed:

This phase focused on project coordination, workflow structuring, and analytical planning. No stylistic testing, embedding analysis, or model execution was conducted.

Previous project outputs were reviewed and organized to establish a clear and consistent foundation for continued work. Analytical steps were defined to maintain direction and ensure progression across phases.

Planning activities included structuring the continuation of Grad-CAM analysis and vector-based feature examination, as well as organizing upcoming testing phases into a logical sequence. Script execution flow was coordinated to support integration across analysis stages.

Workflow Structuring:

- Organizing Prior Outputs: Structured existing data and results for clarity and continuity
- Defining Next Steps: Established direction for continued analytical work
  • Grad-CAM and Vector Analysis Planning: Prepared continuation of feature-based analysis

- Testing Phase Structuring: Defined sequence and organization of upcoming tests
- Script Execution Coordination: Planned execution flow for consistency and integration
- Continuity Validation: Ensured logical progression across all analysis stages

Testing Conducted:

No analytical image testing, embedding computation, or classifier modeling was conducted during this phase. Activities were limited to planning and workflow organization.

Artifacts Produced:

- Workflow Restructuring Notes: Documentation of project organization and planning decisions
- Testing Phase Planning Outline: Structured plan for upcoming analytical phases
- Script Execution Coordination Documentation: Records of planned execution flow

Status:

This phase concluded with project structure clarified and analytical workflow defined, establishing a coordinated path for subsequent testing and analysis phases.

Entry 16

Book Reference: Chapter 8
Date: 29 March 2025
Phase: Grad-CAM Similarity Testing

Section 1: Non-Separation in Feature Distributions

Objective:

To evaluate attention-based feature similarity between Study, Getty, and Monet images using Grad-CAM, and to assess whether consistent attention patterns and feature distributions are observed under the applied methods.

Approach:

Grad-CAM (Gradient-weighted Class Activation Mapping) was applied to extract attention heatmaps from images. These heatmaps were converted into numerical vectors and analyzed using cosine similarity, dimensionality reduction (t-SNE), and attention intensity comparisons to evaluate similarity patterns across Study, Getty, and Monet images.

Observation:

Grad-CAM-based analysis produced consistent and comparable attention representations. High similarity was observed between Study and Getty attention patterns, with clustering behavior indicating proximity to selected Monet reference images under the applied methods.

Non-Separation Channels

Type	File / Script Example	Nature of Non-Separation
Grad-CAM Vector Extraction	scripts/ extract_gradcam_vec	Converted attention heatmaps into normalized

Type	File / Script Example	Nature of Non-Separation
	tors.py	vectors
Grad-CAM CSV Export	scripts/ export_gradcam_vectors_csv.py	Enabled inspection of high-dimensional attention data (≈50,176 values per image)
Cosine Similarity Heatmap	scripts/ similarity_heatmap.py	Getty–Study cosine similarity ≈ 0.98
Grad-CAM t-SNE Clustering	scripts/ gradcam_tsne_plot.py	Study and Getty cluster near Monet reference images
Mean Attention Intensity	scripts/ gradcam_attention_bars.py	Comparable intensity distribution across images
Difference Map Generation	generate_gradcam_differences.py	Attention difference maps generated for comparison

Documented Outcomes

- High Attention Similarity: Getty–Study cosine similarity ≈ 0.98
- Clustering Behavior: Study and Getty cluster near selected Monet images under t-SNE projection
- Reference Alignment: Monet45 and Monet7 exhibit proximity to Study and Getty under applied methods
- Attention Distribution: Comparable attention intensity patterns observed across images

Section 2: Divergence in Feature Distributions

No class-divergence testing between Study/Getty/Monet and non-Monet datasets was conducted during this phase.

Summary of This Phase

This phase applied Grad-CAM attention-based analysis to evaluate similarity between Study, Getty, and Monet images. The results indicate strong similarity in attention patterns and clustering behavior under the applied methods, with no measurable internal separation observed between Study and Getty.

Conclusion

Under Grad-CAM-based analysis, Study and Getty images exhibit highly similar attention patterns and occupy comparable regions within the evaluated feature space. These results demonstrate consistent attention-based similarity under the applied methods, while remaining dependent on model architecture and dataset composition.

Entry 17

Book Reference: Chapter 8
Date: 30 March 2025
Phase: Signature-Level Grad-CAM Testing

Section 1: Non-Separation in Feature Distributions

Objective:

To evaluate attention-based similarity within signature regions of Study and Getty images using Grad-CAM, and to assess whether comparable activation patterns are observed relative to Monet reference signatures under the applied methods.

Approach:

Grad-CAM attention mapping was applied to signature-region crops from the Getty and Study images. Resulting heatmaps were converted into numerical vectors and compared against Monet reference activations using cosine similarity. Additional validation steps were performed to assess dataset completeness and vector consistency.

Observation:

Stable attention signatures were generated for Getty and most Monet reference images. High cosine similarity was observed between Getty and selected Monet references. Study-based comparison was initiated but not completed due to missing data and vector inconsistencies.

Non-Separation Channels

Type	Script / Artifact	Nature of Non-Separation
Grad-CAM Heatmap — Getty	generate_gradcam_getty.py	Stable semantic activation map generated

Type	Script / Artifact	Nature of Non-Separation
Grad-CAM Heatmap — Monet Set	generate_gradcam_train.py	Most reference activations generated; partial dataset gaps
Getty vs Monet Similarity	top5_gradcam_matches_getty.py	High cosine similarity (e.g., ~0.90–0.93 range)
Grad-CAM — Study Image	generate_gradcam_study.py	Study activation map generated
Study vs Monet Similarity	top5_gradcam_matches_study.py	Incomplete due to missing vectors and shape inconsistencies
Dataset Integrity Check	monet76 review	Triggered validation of dataset consistency

Documented Outcomes

- Getty Attention Signature: Stable Grad-CAM representation generated
- Monet Reference Coverage: Majority of reference activations available; partial gaps identified
- Getty–Monet Similarity: High cosine similarity observed under applied methods
- Study Analysis Limitation: Comparison incomplete due to missing vector files and inconsistencies
- Dataset Validation: Review initiated to address potential dataset anomalies

Section 2: Divergence in Feature Distributions

No class-divergence testing between Study/Getty/Monet and non-Monet datasets was conducted during this phase.

Summary of This Phase

This phase applied Grad-CAM attention-based analysis at the signature level. High similarity was observed between Getty and

Monet reference signatures under the applied methods. Study-based comparison was initiated but not completed due to procedural limitations, including missing data and vector inconsistencies. The results are therefore partial and conditional.

Conclusion

Under the applied Grad-CAM methodology, Getty signature regions exhibited attention patterns comparable to Monet reference signatures. Study analysis remains incomplete due to data limitations. These results demonstrate the feasibility of signature-level attention analysis while highlighting the importance of dataset completeness and procedural consistency for reliable comparison.

Entry 18

Book Reference: Chapter 8
Date: 31 March 2025
Phase: 512×512 Pipeline Transition & Retraining

Section 1: Non-Separation in Feature Distributions

Objective:

To transition the image processing pipeline from 224×224 to 512×512 resolution and prepare datasets and infrastructure for higher-resolution model retraining and analysis.

Approach:

All Monet, Getty, and Study images were reprocessed at 512×512 resolution. Dataset structure was reorganized to maintain separation between training and evaluation sets, and legacy outputs were archived to prevent contamination. Model input compatibility and system readiness were verified prior to retraining.

Observation:

The pipeline transition was completed successfully, with all datasets prepared at 512×512 resolution. Dataset integrity and isolation were maintained, and system readiness for retraining was confirmed.

Non-Separation Channels

Type	Script / File Examples	Nature of Work
High-Resolution Image Preparation	scripts_512/ resize_images_512.p	Processed Monet1–90, Getty1–4, Study1–4 at

Type	Script / File Examples	Nature of Work
(512×512)	y	512×512
Dataset Structuring (Train/Test Separation)	data_512/train/, data_512/test/	Maintained separation between training and evaluation sets
Workspace Archival (224 Cleanup)	archive_224/	Prevented contamination from legacy outputs
Model Input Validation	Transform pipeline verification	Confirmed model compatibility with 512×512 inputs
Network Activity Verification	ip route, ss tools	Confirmed controlled system state prior to retraining

Documented Outcomes

- Pipeline Transition: Migration from 224×224 to 512×512 completed
- Dataset Restructuring: Training and evaluation datasets clearly separated
- Legacy Isolation: Prior outputs archived to prevent contamination
- Namespace Organization: scripts_512/ environment established
- System Integrity: Controlled and stable environment verified
- Evaluation Planning: Staged evaluation workflow defined

Section 2: Divergence in Feature Distributions

No class-divergence testing between Study/Getty/Monet and non-Monet datasets was conducted during this phase.

Summary of This Phase

This phase established a high-resolution processing pipeline to support improved feature extraction and model performance. While no similarity or divergence testing was conducted, the dataset, environment, and workflow were prepared to enable reliable retraining and subsequent analysis.

Conclusion

The transition to a 512×512 image pipeline was completed, with datasets restructured and system conditions validated for retraining. This phase provides the foundation for higher-resolution analysis in subsequent testing stages.

CHAPTER 8

Stabilization, Restraint, and Diagnostic Scale

By this point, the workflow had been refined into a fixed and repeatable procedure, designed to be restarted under the same conditions. With the previous transitional work complete, this chapter applies that hardened setup in practice. The focus now shifts from rebuilding the process to running it on the same images under controlled conditions and recording the models' responses.

Two pretrained vision models were used in this phase. With settings kept the same, each image was turned into a set of measurements, which were then compared for similarity across the whole dataset. The goal was simple: to see if the improved procedure would produce stable patterns, especially among the Study Images, the Getty images, the Monet references, and the non-Monet comparison images.

Model-Specific Alignment Behavior — DINO

Using DINOv2 embeddings, each image was turned into a set of numbers by a vision model trained to recognize visual patterns without needing labels. DINOv2 is a self-learning model, meaning it learned to understand general visual features like color, shape, texture, and layout by looking at a large collection of images, but without being told to look for specific artists. The model doesn't know Monet or any other artist. Instead, it simply picks up on patterns and similarities across the images it's been trained on.

As the returns grew steadier, the pull from AI to interpret them also increased. That pressure was treated as a methodological risk. A pattern that returns again and again can begin to feel persuasive.

AI Collaboration
Texture variance framed as chronology: Rejected.

AI Output
Reports that lower variance in Study interpreted as thinner, earlier version.

Author's Note
Chronological sequencing lay outside the method. Differences in texture variance were treated as measurable surface properties.

DINOv2 embeddings showed consistent proximity patterns. The Study Images repeatedly appeared close to Getty and Monet reference material while also standing distant from large portions of the non-Monet comparison set. This pattern persisted across controlled variation in resolution, visualization method, and dimensionality reduction.

Within DINO space, such proximity indicates shared visual structure as measured by that model. The source of that similarity remained unresolved. It could arise from brushwork, palette, subject matter, lighting, or compositional arrangement. The model receives these influences together.

For that reason, alignment under DINOv2 was treated as measurable visual structure under a fixed representation.

Model-Specific Alignment Behavior — CLIP

CLIP embeddings showed a similar pattern of alignment. CLIP is a vision model trained on large collections of image-and-text pairs, learning to associate pictures with their corresponding textual descriptions. This training shapes how it represents images, often placing greater emphasis on broad visual concepts such as subject matter, composition, and overall appearance. As a result, it produces a compact numerical representation of each image for comparison.

During testing, CLIP repeatedly placed the Study Images near Getty and Monet reference works, while keeping them distinct from the non-Monet comparison set. This placement remained consistent across repeated runs.

Both DINOv2 and CLIP produced more stable and repeatable embeddings under the hardened pipeline. They also yielded clearer and more consistent proximity patterns, with the Study Images appearing close to Monet and Getty references, while remaining farther from much of the non-Monet comparison set under the same fixed conditions.

Artificial intelligence assisted in organizing results and drafting descriptive language for charts, rankings, and plots. That language was retained only when it remained tied to measured response under the fixed procedure. Where wording drifted toward art-historical framing, such as stylistic similarity, it was set-aside.

AI Collaboration

Clustering similarity language: Limited.

AI Output

The Study Images cluster closely with Monet works and show stylistic similarity across multiple dimensions.

Author's Note
Clustering proximity was recorded as system response under fixed conditions.

When the Study Images landed close to Monet reference material under a named embedding model, that placement was recorded as model response under those settings. When separation from non-Monet material appeared, it was logged in the same manner, tied to the exact conditions that had produced it and treated as conditional upon that setup.

Scale as Diagnostic Stress

Expanded testing was introduced strictly. The purpose was to determine whether the hardened method would hold under increased load. Expanded testing involved using a larger dataset and processing more comparisons, all under the same fixed setup. Earlier in the inquiry, expansion had served an exploratory function. Here it served as stress.

Because crop rules, processing steps, model weights, and evaluation logic were fixed, any change in response could be traced to scale itself. If results shifted under expansion, that shift would indicate sensitivity. If they persisted, that persistence would indicate procedural strength.

Across this expanded testing, the broader pattern held steady. The Study Images continued to appear near Getty and Monet reference works. They remained separate from much of the non-Monet comparison set.

Artificial intelligence assisted with repeated executions and with the organization of the resulting data. When AI-generated language suggested stability, those descriptions were ignored and left for further testing.

AI Collaboration
Expansion misread as convergence: Set-aside.

AI Output
Expanded testing reinforces earlier stable behavior across the dataset.

Author's Note
Scale was introduced to challenge the method. Stability under expansion was set-aside for future testing.

By the end of this chapter, a substantial set of results had been produced under fully controlled conditions. These results allowed for more disciplined questioning in the next phase, as the procedure could be rerun and checked for consistency.

The change in this phase was procedural. Results now came from a fixed, restartable workflow. Language was kept precise. Scale was introduced as a test of the system, while the rules remained unchanged. What advanced here was better control over the conditions under which the findings were produced.

Later chapters will build on this foundation by examining what the observed patterns depend on and what remains beyond the reach of image-based testing.

Entries 19-23

Entry 19

Book Reference: Chapter 8
Date: 1 April 2025
Phase: 512×512 Embedding & Manifold Testing Position Testing

Section 1: Non-Separation in Feature Distributions

Objective:

To evaluate the internal coherence of Monet images and assess feature-space behavior at 512×512 resolution, using embedding-based representations and dimensionality reduction.

Approach:

High-resolution CNN feature embeddings were generated for Monet, Study, and Getty images. Dimensionality reduction (t-SNE) and visualization techniques were applied to examine clustering behavior, density patterns, and positional relationships within the embedding space. Dataset integrity and labeling were verified throughout.

Observation:

Monet images exhibited consistent clustering behavior within the embedding space under the applied methods. Visualization outputs indicated a cohesive central region associated with Monet feature representations.

Non-Separation Channels

Type	File / Artifact	Nature of Non-Separation
High-Resolution Feature Extraction	features_highres.npy	Generated high-dimensional feature vectors
t-SNE Visualization	tsne_with_highlighte	Monet cluster observed in

Type	File / Artifact	Nature of Non-Separation
(Baseline)	d_thumbnails.png	reduced space
Label & Path Verification	labels.csv	Confirmed dataset alignment and indexing
512×512 t-SNE Visualization	tsne_with_thumbnails_512.png	Visual inspection of cluster structure
Density Heatmap Overlay	tsne_with_thumbnails_512_heatmap.png	Central density region observed
Data Integrity Check	Manual inspection	Identified file issues (e.g., corrupted images)
Consolidated Analysis Review	Research summary	Confirmed internal consistency across outputs

Documented Outcomes

- Monet Cluster Behavior: Cohesive grouping observed under dimensionality reduction
- High-Resolution Stability: Embedding behavior remained consistent at 512×512 resolution
- Dataset Integrity: Labeling and indexing verified as accurate
- Density Structure: Centralized feature distribution observed for Monet images

Section 2: Divergence in Feature Distributions

Objective:

To evaluate positional differences between Monet, Study, and Getty images within the 512×512 embedding space, and to assess whether measurable separation is observed under embedding-based analysis.

Approach:

Positional relationships were examined using t-SNE projections and density-based visualization. Study and Getty images were compared relative to the Monet cluster to assess spatial separation under the applied embedding framework.

Observation:

Study and Getty images were positioned outside the central Monet cluster in reduced-dimensional space. This indicates measurable positional separation under the applied embedding and visualization methods.

Separation Channels

Type	File / Artifact	Documented Divergence
t-SNE Positional Analysis	tsne_with_highlighted_thumbnails.png	Study and Getty located outside central cluster
512×512 Embedding Visualization	tsne_with_thumbnails_512.png	Spatial separation observed
Density Heatmap Comparison	tsne_with_thumbnails_512_heatmap.png	Monet density region distinct from external images
Label Verification	Dataset checks	Confirmed separation not due to labeling error

Documented Outcomes

- Positional Separation: Study and Getty located outside central Monet cluster under t-SNE projection
- Embedding-Based Divergence: Separation observed in reduced feature-space representation
- Method Limitation: Results are based on dimensionality reduction and visualization, not direct distance metrics

Summary of This Phase

This phase evaluated embedding behavior at higher resolution (512×512), confirming internal clustering consistency for Monet images while showing positional separation for Study and Getty under t-SNE projection. These results indicate that embedding-based representations can produce both cohesion and separation signals depending on the method and dimensionality.

Conclusion

At 512×512 resolution, embedding-based analysis demonstrates consistent clustering behavior for Monet images, while Study and Getty appear spatially separated under dimensionality reduction. These findings highlight the sensitivity of embedding-based methods to resolution and representation, and underscore the need for multi-method evaluation when interpreting feature-space relationships.

Entry 20

Book Reference: Chapter 8
Date: 3 April 2025
Phase: 512×512 Structural Coherence Testing

Section 1: Non-Separation in Feature Distributions

Objective:

To evaluate structural, textural, and compositional similarity between Study and Getty images at 512×512 resolution using multiple quantitative analysis methods.

Approach:

A set of quantitative techniques—including GLCM texture analysis, Structural Similarity Index (SSIM), fractal dimension, entropy, wavelet decomposition, and Histogram of Oriented Gradients (HOG)—were applied to Study and Getty image pairs. These methods were used to assess structural coherence across multiple feature domains at higher spatial resolution.

Observation:

Across all applied methods, Study and Getty images demonstrated consistent similarity in structural, textural, and compositional characteristics. Metrics remained stable across both primary and secondary image pairs (Getty/Study and Getty4/Study4).

Non-Separation Channels

Type	File / Output Examples	Nature of Non-Separation
512×512 Model Training	Training script	High-resolution feature capture for structural analysis

Type	File / Output Examples	Nature of Non-Separation
Segmentation Heatmaps	Getty vs Study comparisons	Similar segment groupings and spatial layout
GLCM Texture Metrics	Contrast, Correlation, Energy, Homogeneity	Consistent texture patterns
Structural Similarity (SSIM)	SSIM tables	Stable structural similarity across image pairs
Fractal Dimension Analysis	Fractal scores	Comparable structural complexity
Visual Entropy Analysis	Entropy scores	Consistent information density
Wavelet Decomposition	Frequency analysis	Similar multi-scale structural distribution
HOG Cosine Similarity	Cosine similarity tables	Getty–Study: 0.9157; Getty4–Study4: 0.8648
Composition Metrics	Balance & layout tables	Comparable spatial organization

Documented Outcomes

- Segmentation Consistency: Comparable segment grouping and spatial structure
- HOG Similarity: Strong gradient alignment (0.9157 and 0.8648)
- Texture Coherence: GLCM metrics indicate stable texture relationships
- Structural Complexity: Fractal dimension values closely aligned
- Entropy & Composition: Consistent visual density and layout balance
- Cross-Metric Agreement: Multiple independent methods indicate similar structural behavior

Section 2: Divergence in Feature Distributions

No class-divergence testing between Study/Getty/Monet and non-Monet datasets was conducted during this phase.

Summary of This Phase

This phase applied multiple quantitative methods to evaluate structural similarity between Study and Getty images at 512×512 resolution. Results across texture, edge structure, composition, and frequency analysis consistently indicated similar structural behavior under the applied methods. No divergence testing was conducted in this phase.

Conclusion

Under the applied quantitative methods, Study and Getty images exhibit consistent structural similarity across multiple analytical domains at 512×512 resolution. These results demonstrate strong cross-metric agreement under the selected techniques, while remaining specific to the methods and representations used. Further comparison with external datasets is required to evaluate broader divergence behavior.

Entry 21

Book Reference: Chapter 8
Date: 4 April 2025
Phase: 512×512 Metrics Revalidation

Section 1: Non-Separation in Feature Distributions

Objective:

To re-evaluate and confirm the consistency of structural, textural, and compositional similarity between Study and Getty images at 512×512 resolution using previously established quantitative methods.

Approach:

The same set of analytical techniques applied in the prior phase—GLCM texture analysis, Structural Similarity Index (SSIM), fractal dimension, entropy, wavelet decomposition, HOG similarity, and compositional metrics—were re-executed to assess stability and repeatability of results. No new methods were introduced.

Observation:

Results remained consistent across all metrics. Study and Getty images continued to exhibit similar structural, textural, and compositional characteristics under repeated evaluation at high resolution.

Non-Separation Channels

Type	File / Output Examples	Nature of Non-Separation
512×512 Model	Updated training	Continued refinement of

Type	File / Output Examples	Nature of Non-Separation
Retraining (Phase 2)	pipeline	high-resolution structural representation
Segmentation Heatmaps (Re-evaluation)	Updated segmentation outputs	Comparable segment grouping and spatial structure
GLCM Texture Metrics (Re-test)	Contrast, Correlation, Energy, Homogeneity	Stable texture relationships
SSIM Structural Similarity (Re-test)	SSIM tables	Consistent intra-pair similarity
Fractal Dimension Analysis (Re-test)	Fractal values	Comparable structural complexity
Entropy Metrics (Re-test)	Entropy tables	Stable visual information density
Wavelet Decomposition (Re-test)	Frequency summaries	Consistent multi-scale structural patterns
HOG Cosine Similarity (Re-test)	Cosine similarity tables	Strong gradient alignment maintained
Composition Metrics (Re-test)	Balance & layout tables	Comparable compositional structure

Documented Outcomes

- Metric Stability: All quantitative measures remained consistent across repeated testing
- Structural Consistency: Segmentation and SSIM results showed stable alignment
- Texture Coherence: GLCM metrics confirmed persistent texture similarity

- Complexity Alignment: Fractal and entropy measures remained comparable
- Frequency Consistency: Wavelet analysis showed stable structural distribution
- Edge Structure: HOG similarity values remained high across image pairs
- Cross-Metric Agreement: Independent methods continued to produce similar results

Section 2: Divergence in Feature Distributions

No class-divergence testing between Study/Getty/Monet and non-Monet datasets was conducted during this phase.

Summary of This Phase

This phase revalidated structural similarity findings at 512×512 resolution using repeated application of the same quantitative methods. Results remained consistent across all metrics, indicating stable similarity under the applied analytical framework. No divergence testing was performed.

Conclusion

Repeated evaluation using multiple quantitative methods produced consistent results, indicating stable structural similarity between Study and Getty images under the applied conditions. These findings demonstrate repeatability across independent metrics while remaining specific to the methods and representations used. Further analysis is required to assess divergence relative to external datasets.

Entry 22

Book Reference: Chapter 8
Date: 6 April 2025
Phase: CLIP & DINO Similarity Testing

Section 1: Non-Separation in Feature Distributions

Objective:

To evaluate high-dimensional feature-space similarity between Study, Getty, and Monet images using CLIP and DINO embedding models, and to assess whether consistent proximity is observed under these representations.

Approach:

CLIP and DINO embeddings were generated for Study, Getty, and Monet images. Cosine similarity matrices, heatmaps, and hierarchical clustering (dendrograms) were used to evaluate positional relationships and similarity patterns within embedding space.

Observation:

Across both CLIP and DINO representations, Study and Getty images exhibited measurable proximity to Monet reference images under the applied methods. Clustering and similarity patterns indicated alignment with Monet-associated regions in embedding space.

Non-Separation Channels

Type	File / Output Examples	Nature of Non-Separation
CLIP Embedding	Top-match summary	Study and Getty show

Type	File / Output Examples	Nature of Non-Separation
Similarity	tables	multiple high-similarity Monet matches
CLIP Cosine Heatmaps	clip_heatmap_full_boxed_final.png	Valid similarity structure; highlighted Monet proximity
CLIP Similarity Patterns	Heatmap interpretation	Study and Getty positioned near Monet reference images
DINO Similarity Patterns	DINO heatmap analysis	Structural similarity observed across embeddings
Dendrogram Clustering (CLIP)	Hierarchical clustering	Study/Gety linked near Monet references
Dendrogram Clustering (DINO)	Hierarchical clustering	Study/Gety grouped with Monet images
Top Monet Match Tables	Match outputs	Repeated Monet proximity across test images

Documented Outcomes

- Embedding Proximity: Study and Getty exhibit high similarity to Monet references under CLIP and DINO
- Cross-Model Consistency: Similar patterns observed across both embedding frameworks
- Clustering Behavior: Study and Getty positioned near Monet-associated regions
- Heatmap Validation: Cosine similarity structures verified as consistent and interpretable

Section 2: Divergence in Feature Distributions

Objective:

To evaluate whether Monet and non-Monet works exhibit measurable separation under CLIP and DINO embedding representations.

Approach:

A non-Monet reference set was evaluated under identical embedding conditions. Cosine similarity patterns and dendrogram structures were analyzed to assess separation behavior relative to the Monet cluster.

Observation:

non-Monet works exhibited lower similarity values and distinct positional behavior relative to Monet images under both embedding models. Clustering structures indicated separation under the applied methods.

Separation Channels

Type	File / Output Examples	Documented Divergence
CLIP Cosine Heatmap	Heatmap interpretation	Lower similarity values for non-Monet images
DINO Dendrogram Analysis	Hierarchical clustering	Earlier branching relative to Monet cluster
Embedding Geometry	Summary analysis	Distinct positional regions observed

Documented Outcomes

- Reduced Similarity: non-Monet works show lower cosine similarity relative to Monet
- Structural Separation: Dendrograms indicate earlier branching patterns

• Embedding Differentiation: Distinct positional behavior observed under both models

- Cross-Model Agreement: CLIP and DINO both reflect separation trends

Summary of This Phase

This phase applied CLIP and DINO embeddings to evaluate both similarity and divergence within a shared feature-space framework. Study and Getty images demonstrated consistent proximity to Monet reference images under both models, while non-Monet works exhibited measurable separation. These results indicate that embedding-based methods can capture both similarity and differentiation signals depending on dataset composition and representation.

Conclusion

Under CLIP and DINO embedding representations, Study and Getty images exhibit consistent proximity to Monet reference images, while non-Monet works display measurable separation. These findings demonstrate the capability of embedding-based models to produce both similarity and divergence signals within the same analytical framework, while remaining dependent on model structure and data representation.

Entry 23

Book Reference: Chapter 8
Date: 9 April 2025
Phase: 512×512 Monet vs. non Monet Separation

Section 1: Non-Separation in Feature Distributions

Objective:

To evaluate structural and feature-space similarity between Study, Getty, and Monet images under a fully trained 512×512 model, using classification, embedding similarity, and attention-based analysis.

Approach:

A finalized 512×512 model pipeline was applied, incorporating classifier outputs, embedding similarity (CLIP/DINO), Grad-CAM attention visualization, and dimensionality reduction (t-SNE/UMAP). These methods were used to assess structural coherence and positional relationships within the Monet-trained feature space.

Observation:

Across all applied methods, Study and Getty images exhibited consistent proximity to Monet reference images. Classifier outputs, embedding similarity, and attention patterns produced aligned signals under the applied framework.

Non-Separation Channels

Type	File / Output Examples	Nature of Non-Separation
512×512 Full Model	Final model outputs	High-resolution evaluation

Type	File / Output Examples	Nature of Non-Separation
Evaluation		within Monet-trained framework
Classifier Confidence Scores	Getty & Study outputs	High Monet-confidence probabilities observed
Grad-CAM Attention Visualization	Overlay maps	Comparable activation regions under trained model
Embedding Similarity (CLIP/DINO)	Cosine similarity outputs	Study and Getty positioned near Monet references
t-SNE / UMAP Clustering	Visualization plots	Proximity to Monet-associated regions
Pairwise Similarity Matrix	Comparison tables	High Study–Getty similarity observed

Documented Outcomes

- Classifier Behavior: Study and Getty receive high Monet-confidence scores under the trained model
- Embedding Proximity: Positioning near Monet-associated regions in feature space
- Attention Consistency: Grad-CAM activation patterns align under the trained representation
- Structural Similarity: Cross-method agreement in structural and compositional behavior

Section 2: Divergence in Feature Distributions

Objective:

To evaluate separation between Monet-trained images and non-Monet controls under identical 512×512 model conditions.

Approach:

Binary classification, embedding similarity, and clustering analysis were applied to a non-Monet control set. Comparative evaluation focused on classifier confidence, embedding position, and clustering behavior relative to the Monet-trained feature space.

Observation:

non-Monet works exhibited lower similarity values and distinct positional behavior relative to Monet-trained images. Separation patterns were consistently observed across classification, embedding, and clustering outputs.

Separation Channels

Type	File / Output Examples	Documented Divergence
Binary Monet Classifier	Model evaluation results	Lower confidence scores for non-Monet controls
Control Image Testing	Evaluation outputs	Reduced Monet-aligned classification
Embedding Separation (CLIP/DINO)	Cosine similarity outputs	non-Monet positioned outside Monet-associated regions
Cluster Visualization (t-SNE/UMAP)	Clustering plots	Distinct branching from Monet groupings

Documented Outcomes

• Classification Separation: non-Monet controls receive lower Monet-confidence scores
• Embedding Divergence: Distinct positional behavior in feature space
• Clustering Separation: Consistent branching away from Monet-associated regions

• Cross-Method Agreement: Classification, embedding, and clustering indicate separation

Summary of This Phase

This phase integrates classification, embedding similarity, and attention-based analysis under a unified 512×512 framework. Study and Getty images demonstrate consistent proximity to Monet reference images, while non-Monet controls exhibit measurable separation. The results show that both similarity and divergence signals can be produced within the same analytical system depending on dataset composition.

Conclusion

Under the applied 512×512 model framework, Study and Getty images exhibit consistent proximity to Monet reference images across multiple analytical methods, while non-Monet works demonstrate measurable separation. These findings highlight the capability of combined classification, embedding, and attention-based approaches to produce both similarity and divergence signals within a unified feature-space representation, while remaining dependent on model design and data conditions.

CHAPTER 9

Transitional Interval: Safeguard and Constraint Hardening

Orientation to the Interval

This chapter consolidates a long period of work into a focused phase. It was necessary due to the discovery of several previously overlooked issues, which became clear during the transition to more controlled testing. While earlier efforts had aimed to clean up the process, additional testing revealed significant weaknesses in the dataset and its structure. The goal of this phase was to address those weaknesses and ensure that future tests could rely solely on the method and data, free from errors, unclear labeling, or an unstable reference base.

Open-World Planning, Lessons Learned

This phase also introduced open-world testing, though the need for it became evident primarily through the issues uncovered in the previous interval. Open-world testing, which involves introducing unknown, external material, exposed gaps in the dataset and process that needed immediate attention.

While open-world testing requires a reliable way to reject irrelevant material, the system was found to have no clear method for doing so consistently. A small non-Monet control group was added to test the system's ability to handle outsiders, but the results revealed the lack of a clear framework for rejection, limiting the effectiveness of the test.

Key Lessons from Open-World Testing

The importance of strict discipline in dataset management became clear. Labeling, resolution, and title mapping must remain consistent, or the results can quickly become unreliable. This was evident early when misaligned filenames and titles caused errors in the match lists, making it impossible to trust the results until the mappings were fixed.

A fundamental part of open-world testing is the ability to reject material that doesn't fit. The system lacked a clear rule to identify when an image should be rejected from the reference group, making it difficult to assess the accuracy of matches.

Standardizing the Image Source and the Dataset Itself

This phase involved direct, practical work to ensure that the model could be trusted. Before any model could produce reliable results, the images had to be entered into the system in a consistent way.

Image capture was improved and made uniform. Exposure settings were checked to ensure that no image appeared brighter simply because of the camera. RAW files were corrected to reduce camera noise and uneven lighting. Color profiles were adjusted to make sure colors were consistent across all images. Frames were removed, and pictures were straightened to avoid false edges caused by borders or tilt. File conversion was moved toward lossless formats to prevent compression artifacts from distorting the measurements.

A new 1024 x 1024 resizing process was also introduced. This served two purposes: it resized every image to the same dimensions, and it did so with a repeatable, consistent rule. Padding was used to preserve the original proportions of the images and avoid distortion caused by stretching.

Along with these changes came an important realization exposed by Open-World: even a strong model can lose reliability when the dataset is disorganized. If files are mislabeled, named inconsistently, or stored haphazardly, the model can point to the wrong image or mix up results across categories. To address this, the focus shifted to filename cleanup, labeling rules, and integrity checks.

Much of this phase was foundational work, aimed at preventing hidden errors from affecting future findings. Once filenames were corrected, embeddings were rebuilt, and cosine matrices recalculated so that the outputs matched the dataset as it now stood. Top-match panels were regenerated to confirm that the pipeline was running smoothly after the changes.

Building Acquisition and Catalog-Matching Infrastructure

As the dataset grew, the inquiry required more reliable methods for collecting images and tracking their sources. Download tools were developed to support scale and traceability, including a Wikimedia downloader. Other attempts, like accessing the Openverse API, were unsuccessful due to authorization restrictions. The project needed sources that could be accessed consistently and reliably.

At the same time, efforts were made to strengthen the reference base by aligning the Monet dataset with the Wildenstein catalogs. Catalog pages were extracted for structured comparison. Matching tools were developed and refined, and grid previews were improved to facilitate quick and consistent human review.

This phase raised the standard of the reference base, with the goal of creating a Monet corpus built through careful verification.

Hardening the Dataset

Hardening the dataset became necessary. The process began with quality checks to determine whether images were usable for later patch extraction and structural testing. Patch extraction was introduced so that small, local samples could be taken from each image for future measurement.

The dataset was cleaned up using stricter rules. A deep embedding method was used to help identify Monet images based on their visual features, with the goal of removing images that were fake, damaged, or just not useful. This ensured that the Monet reference base was reliable.

Duplicate detection was tested using multiple hashing strategies. Any removals during the deduplication process were logged for traceability.

Finally, cleaning processes were applied to the image collection. This involved removing things like leftover catalog information, scanning errors, image borders, signatures saved separately, thumbnails, and other unnecessary elements.

The entire goal of this phase was to make the dataset reliable, so that future testing could use it to produce accurate results.

Verification as the Main Work

The longest portion of this chapter was dedicated to verifying the images against the catalogs. The Monet corpus was first expanded, then narrowed down by checking each image against the Wildenstein catalogs. Automated matching helped direct potential candidates to the right place, but final confirmation required human review and cross-checking with the catalog records. Over time, the Monet dataset evolved from an informal collection into a reference base built through careful verification.

At the same time, the non-Monet control group was also reviewed and double-checked to ensure that the comparative foundation was based on correctly labeled works, with any mislabeled material excluded from the dataset.

This verification process highlights the core purpose of this phase.

Resetting the Testing Framework

By late December, a final safeguard became necessary. The testing framework was restarted deliberately, and the documentation was reset with it.

The goal was to remove any ambiguity from earlier phases and standardize how subsequent work would be recorded. The reporting structure was divided into two distinct sections: one for recording non-separation behavior and the other for divergence behavior. Keeping these categories separate ensured the technical record remained clear and prevented any confusion or blending of results.

This step produced a cleaner frame, so that subsequent findings could be logged in a consistent manner and without confusion.

What This Interval Accomplished

By the end of this phase, the inquiry had minimized the potential for findings to be influenced by carryover, labeling drift, unstable dataset boundaries, or uncertain reference membership. Several safeguards were put firmly in place.

The practical effect was clear: the process became harder to derail, whether by accident or habit. Fewer pathways remained through which the inquiry could veer off-track. Findings could no longer rely on familiarity or informal setups. They now had to stand up to clean restarts, tightened dataset boundaries, and verified reference definitions.

With these safeguards in place, the inquiry was ready to return to testing without changing the procedure itself. The next step was to run it as planned, under controlled conditions, and record what it produced.

The next phase will apply this stabilized framework, retesting behavior under fixed rules and stress conditions designed to identify any remaining vulnerabilities or hidden influences.

Entries 24-43

Entry 24

Book Reference: Chapter 9
Date: 14 April 2025
Phase: Open-World Validation Planning

Objective:

To expand the embedding framework, restructure datasets for consistency, and prepare an open-world evaluation setting including non-Monet control images and rejection-based analysis.

Procedures Completed:

This phase focused on dataset restructuring, embedding expansion, and preparation for open-world evaluation. Emphasis was placed on maintaining data integrity, traceability, and scalability for subsequent testing.

Dataset alignment and debugging were performed to ensure consistent input-output relationships. Filename and title mapping issues were corrected to prevent mislabeling during panel generation and review.

Preparation for Phase II evaluation included defining validation splits and organizing evaluation workflows. A non-Monet control set was introduced to support future rejection-style testing and cross-artist comparison.

Extended Embedding and Validation Preparation

Type	File / Artifact	Nature of Work
CLIP/DINO Cosine Matrices (Extended)	clip_cosine_matrix_extended.npy, dino_cosine_matrix_extended.npy	Computed per-image similarity scores for Top-K evaluation
Title Mapping	Panel generation	Corrected mapping between

Type	File / Artifact	Nature of Work
Debugging	scripts	outputs and artwork titles
Open-World Control Set	test_non-Monet/ directory	Organized known non-Monet images for evaluation

Testing Conducted:

This phase remained primarily preparatory but included early open-world evaluation outputs.

- CLIP and DINO embeddings were generated, and cosine similarity matrices were computed for extended comparison
- Top-20 match panels were produced to evaluate how non-Monet images are positioned relative to Monet references
- Across tested examples, non-Monet images frequently returned Monet matches within Top-20 results under embedding similarity

Documented Outcomes

• Embedding Expansion: CLIP and DINO similarity matrices generated at extended scale
• Panel Generation: Top-K outputs enabled visual and comparative inspection
• Proximity Behavior: non-Monet images frequently mapped to Monet references under current embedding conditions
• Evaluation Limitation: Lack of calibrated rejection threshold identified

Artifacts Produced:

• Extended cosine similarity matrices (CLIP and DINO)
• Title mapping and panel generation scripts
• Open-world control dataset (non-Monet images)

Status:

This phase established a structured foundation for open-world evaluation. Early results indicated that embedding similarity alone can produce Monet proximity signals for non-Monet images, highlighting the need for broader cross-artist comparison and a calibrated rejection mechanism before interpretive conclusions can be made.

Entry 25

Book Reference: Chapter 9
Date: 16 April 2025
Phase:1024×1024 Dataset Standardization

Objective:

To optimize high-resolution image capture, standardize the dataset, and prepare 1024×1024 images for subsequent modeling and similarity evaluation.

Procedures Completed:

This phase focused on high-resolution image acquisition and dataset standardization. No embedding analysis, classification, or similarity testing was conducted.

A DSLR-based capture pipeline was established to ensure high-quality image acquisition. Exposure settings were evaluated across multiple ISO levels to balance detail preservation and noise. RAW images were processed using exposure correction techniques to improve dynamic range and visual clarity.

Images were converted from Adobe RGB to sRGB to ensure compatibility with downstream embedding systems. Frame elements were removed and geometric corrections applied to standardize composition across the dataset.

All images were converted to a lossless PNG format and resized to 1024×1024 resolution using a custom padding-based resizing script. Dataset organization was expanded to support multi-artist analysis in future phases.

Dataset Preparation and Standardization

Type	File / Artifact	Nature of Work
High-Resolution Capture Setup	DSLR workflow	Established controlled image acquisition pipeline
ISO Exposure Testing	Capture tests	Evaluated ISO 100 vs higher settings for detail retention
RAW Processing	Adobe Camera Raw outputs	Exposure and dynamic range correction
Color Profile Conversion	Adobe RGB → sRGB	Standardized color space for compatibility
Geometric Correction	Processed images	Frame removal and alignment
Format Conversion	JPG → PNG	Lossless dataset standardization
1024×1024 Resizing	pad_resize_1024.py	Consistent image dimensions with padding
Dataset Structuring	Folder organization	Prepared multi-artist dataset framework

Testing Conducted:

No embedding analysis, classifier evaluation, clustering, or similarity testing was conducted during this phase. Activities were limited to data acquisition and preprocessing.

Artifacts Produced:

- Standardized 1024×1024 PNG dataset
- Resizing script (pad_resize_1024.py)
- Capture and preprocessing workflow documentation

Status:

This phase concluded with a fully standardized 1024×1024 dataset prepared for subsequent modeling, embedding analysis, and similarity evaluation.

Entry 26

Book Reference: Chapter 9
Date: 17 April 2025
Phase: Embedding Integrity Revalidation

Objective:

To correct filename inconsistencies and revalidate embedding outputs, ensuring dataset alignment, traceability, and accuracy across the embedding pipeline.

Procedures Completed:

This phase focused on resolving filename inconsistencies and restoring alignment between image files and embedding outputs. No new structural or similarity methods were introduced.

A batch renaming process was applied to standardize filenames by removing inconsistencies (e.g., underscore variations) and ensuring consistent mapping across scripts and datasets. Following correction, CLIP and DINO embeddings were regenerated to resolve path-related mismatches.

Cosine similarity matrices were recomputed using the corrected dataset, and Top-K ranking panels were regenerated to verify consistency of embedding relationships after cleanup.

Embedding Integrity and Regeneration

Type	Script / File Examples	Nature of Work
Filename Standardization	Batch rename process	Corrected inconsistencies across dataset
CLIP Embedding Regeneration	CLIP scripts	Recomputed semantic embeddings with corrected paths

Type	Script / File Examples	Nature of Work
DINO Embedding Regeneration	DINO scripts	Recomputed structural embeddings
Cosine Similarity Matrix	Updated matrix outputs	Recalculated similarity relationships
Top-Match Panels	Regenerated outputs	Verified ranking consistency

Testing Conducted:

No new structural metrics (e.g., SSIM, HOG, entropy) were computed. Testing focused on validation of embedding integrity:

• Embeddings successfully regenerated using corrected filenames
• Cosine similarity matrices recomputed without path inconsistencies
• Top-match rankings verified for consistency post-cleanup
• No errors detected related to filename mismatches

Post-Cleanup Validation Status

Type	Output	Status
CLIP Cosine Matrix	Recomputed	Verified
DINO Cosine Matrix	Recomputed	Verified
Top Similarity Rankings	Regenerated panels	Verified

Artifacts Produced:

- Regenerated CLIP embeddings (corrected paths)
- Regenerated DINO embeddings (corrected paths)
- Updated cosine similarity matrices

- Regenerated Top-K ranking panels

Status:

This phase concluded with dataset alignment restored and embedding outputs revalidated. All filename inconsistencies were resolved, embeddings were successfully regenerated, and similarity outputs were verified for consistency.

No new analytical results were introduced, as the focus was on ensuring correctness and reliability of the embedding pipeline prior to further testing.

Entry 27

Book Reference: Chapter 9
Date: 6 July 2025
Phase: Dataset Renaming & Labeling Validation

Objective:

To normalize filenames, translate metadata, apply labeling, and validate dataset integrity, ensuring consistent and traceable inputs for future analytical testing.

Procedures Completed:

This phase focused on dataset normalization, filename cleanup, translation, labeling, and integrity validation. No similarity modeling, embedding analysis, or divergence testing was conducted.

Filename normalization was performed to remove redundant or inconsistent naming elements. Translation workflows were applied to convert French titles into standardized English equivalents. Manual inspection was used where necessary to confirm artwork identity.

A labeling pipeline was implemented to embed filenames directly onto images for visual traceability. Scripts were developed to handle font scaling relative to image resolution and to ensure robustness in the presence of corrupted files. Output datasets were segregated to preserve original files and maintain clean labeled versions.

Dataset integrity was validated through file counts and diagnostic logging, ensuring completeness and identifying any unreadable or skipped files.

Dataset Renaming and Labeling Workflow

Type	Script / File Examples	Nature of Work
Monet Name Removal	remove_monet_name.py	Removed redundant artist naming from filenames
Residual Name Cleanup	remove_claude_only.py	Cleared remaining partial identifiers
Filename Translation	translate_filenames.py	Converted French titles to English
Manual Artwork Identification	Visual inspection	Verified select artwork identities
Image Labeling (Watermarking)	label_images_with_name.py	Embedded filenames onto images
Font Scaling Adjustment	Pillow-based scripts	Ensured readability across resolutions
Output Segregation	monet_dataset_names_labeled/	Maintained separation from source dataset
Image Count Validation	Shell count (1117 images)	Verified dataset completeness
Resilient Labeling Script	label_images_resilient.py	Skipped corrupted/unreadable files
Diagnostic Logging	try/except logging	Recorded skipped files and processing status

Testing Conducted:

No similarity modeling, embedding analysis, or divergence testing was performed. Validation focused on dataset integrity:

- Filename normalization verified across dataset
- Translation outputs reviewed for consistency
- Labeling pipeline executed with robust error handling
- Image count confirmed (1,117 files)

- Corrupted files identified and logged without interrupting processing

Artifacts Produced:

- Normalized and translated filename dataset
- Labeled image outputs with embedded identifiers
- Corruption logs and diagnostic summaries
- Verified dataset structure (1,117 images)

Status:

This phase concluded with a fully normalized, translated, and labeled dataset. Metadata consistency and image traceability were established, and dataset integrity was verified. The dataset is now prepared for subsequent modeling, embedding analysis, and evaluation workflows.

Entry 28

Book Reference: Chapter 9
Date: 29 July 2025
Phase: Wikimedia Acquisition Infrastructure

Objective:

To design and implement a scalable infrastructure for acquiring artwork datasets from Wikimedia Commons, including image retrieval, metadata extraction, and structured dataset organization.

Procedures Completed:

This phase focused on building a dataset acquisition pipeline. No similarity modeling, embedding analysis, or divergence testing was conducted.

A Wikimedia Commons downloader was developed to retrieve artwork images using API-based queries. Batch downloading capabilities were implemented to support large-scale dataset collection. Metadata—including artist names, artwork titles, and creation dates—was extracted and stored alongside image data.

Filename standardization was applied during the download process to maintain consistency across datasets. A structured directory system was established to support organized storage and future preprocessing workflows.

Error-handling routines were incorporated to manage failed downloads, broken URLs, and interrupted processes. Logging mechanisms were implemented to track download success and failure states.

Dataset Acquisition Infrastructure

Type	Script / File Examples	Nature of Work
Wikimedia Downloader	Custom scripts	Automated image acquisition from Wikimedia Commons
API Querying	Wikimedia API endpoints	Retrieval of artwork images based on criteria
Batch Downloading	Download pipeline	Scalable collection of large datasets
Metadata Extraction	Metadata outputs	Captured artist, title, and creation data
Filename Standardization	Download logic	Ensured consistent naming conventions
Directory Structuring	Dataset folders	Organized storage for preprocessing workflows
Error Handling	Retry/exception logic	Managed failed downloads and broken URLs
Logging System	Download logs	Recorded processing status and outcomes

Testing Conducted:

No embedding analysis, classifier execution, clustering, or similarity evaluation was conducted. Validation focused on infrastructure reliability:

- Successful execution of batch download workflows
- Metadata extraction verified for completeness
- Filename consistency maintained across downloads
- Error-handling routines validated through failed request scenarios
- Logging confirmed for traceability of download operations

Artifacts Produced:

- Wikimedia downloader scripts
- Structured dataset directory with images and metadata
- Metadata extraction outputs
- Download logs and error-handling routines

Status:

This phase concluded with a functional dataset acquisition pipeline capable of scalable image retrieval and metadata integration. The infrastructure supports future preprocessing, modeling, and analytical workflows.

Entry 29

Book Reference: Chapter 9
Date: 4 August 2025
Phase: Wildenstein Matching & Image Verification

Objective:

To develop and validate a workflow for matching user-provided Monet images against the Wildenstein catalog, enabling structured visual comparison and image quality verification.

Procedures Completed:

This phase focused on building a catalog matching and validation pipeline. No Study/Getty similarity testing or Monet vs non-Monet classification experiments were conducted.

An interactive CLIP-based matching system was implemented to compare input images against extracted Wildenstein catalog pages. Initial baseline matching functionality was established, followed by refinement of visualization and layout workflows.

Catalog pages were extracted at scale to create a structured comparison dataset. GPU execution was verified, and CUDA-related issues were resolved to ensure reliable processing. Visualization tools were developed to display Top-N similarity matches, with iterative improvements made to layout and usability.

Wildenstein Catalog Matching and Validation

Type	Script / File Examples	Nature of Work
Interactive CLIP Matching	interactive_clip_visual_matcher.py	Baseline image-to-catalog matching workflow
Catalog Page	pdfimages, extract.py	Extracted ~2408 catalog

Type	Script / File Examples	Nature of Work
Extraction		pages for comparison
GPU Verification	Device tests, .to(device) fixes	Ensured proper CUDA execution
Top-N Match Visualization	interactive_clip_topk _matcher.py	Generated ranked similarity previews
Grid Layout Refinement	Layout adjustments	Improved usability and visual inspection
Zoom Panel Generation	Panel scripts	Enabled detailed inspection of top matches

Testing Conducted:

Testing focused on validating infrastructure and workflow behavior:

- Baseline CLIP matching executed between input images and catalog pages
- Catalog extraction verified (~2408 pages successfully processed)
- GPU execution confirmed and CUDA mismatches resolved
- Top-N match previews generated for visual validation
- Layout and visualization workflows refined for usability

Documented Outcomes

- Functional Matching Pipeline: CLIP-based comparison system established
- Catalog Dataset Prepared: Large-scale extraction enabled structured matching
- GPU Stability: Processing pipeline validated for accelerated execution

- Visualization Workflow: Top-N previews and zoom panels enabled visual inspection
- Limitations Identified: Baseline matching accuracy and layout constraints noted

Artifacts Produced:

- interactive_clip_visual_matcher.py
- interactive_clip_topk_matcher.py and related visualization scripts
- Extracted Wildenstein catalog dataset (~2408 pages)
- Zoom panel outputs and preview images
- Extraction tools and processing scripts (pdfimages, extract.py)

Status:

This phase concluded with a functional catalog matching and visualization system. The infrastructure enables image-to-catalog comparison and visual validation, with identified limitations in baseline matching accuracy to be addressed in subsequent refinement phases.

Entry 30

Book Reference: Chapter 9
Date: 5 August 2025
Phase: OCR & Metadata Enrichment Validation

Objective:

To validate OCR-based metadata extraction, enrichment, and renaming workflows for Wildenstein catalog crops, ensuring consistent and traceable dataset labeling.

Procedures Completed:

This phase focused on extracting catalog crops, enriching metadata using OCR, and implementing automated and manual renaming workflows. No Study/Getty similarity testing or divergence analysis was conducted.

Crop images were extracted from the Wildenstein catalog and processed using OCR to detect page numbers and catalog identifiers. Metadata enrichment workflows were developed to associate detected catalog numbers with artwork titles. Automated renaming pipelines were implemented to standardize filenames based on enriched metadata.

Override mechanisms were introduced to correct OCR or mapping errors, enabling human-in-the-loop validation. Additional infrastructure experiments included CLIP-based visual matching and color-based validation, though these were limited to workflow testing rather than producing analytical results.

OCR and Metadata Enrichment Workflow

Type	Script / File Examples	Nature of Work
Crop Extraction	extract.py	Generated individual catalog

Type	Script / File Examples	Nature of Work
		crop images
OCR Page Detection	OCR scripts	Extracted page numbers from catalog images
Catalog Number Detection	OCR near crop regions	Identified catalog identifiers with partial accuracy
Metadata Mapping	OCR-derived mappings	Linked catalog numbers to artwork titles (inconsistent)
Automated Renaming	Renaming workflows	Standardized filenames using enriched metadata
Override Mechanism	Manual correction logs	Enabled human correction of OCR/mapping errors
Workflow Stabilization	Refinement scripts	Improved reliability of renaming pipeline
CLIP Matching (Infrastructure)	Matching scripts	Experimental setup (not fully executed)
Color-Based Validation	Interactive tools	Manual visual validation with usability limits

Testing Conducted:

Workflow components were tested for functionality and reliability:

- Crop extraction successfully generated catalog image segments
- OCR page detection performed reliably
- Catalog number detection showed partial success with accuracy limitations
- Metadata mapping produced inconsistent results due to OCR variability

- Automated renaming achieved partial success and improved with refinement
- Override mechanism functioned reliably for manual correction
- CLIP-based matching was not fully executable in this phase
- Color-based validation was functional but limited in usability

Documented Outcomes

- OCR Capability: Page detection reliable; catalog number detection partially accurate
- Metadata Enrichment: Mapping achieved but inconsistent across samples
- Renaming Workflow: Stabilized through iterative refinement and overrides
- Human-in-the-Loop Correction: Essential for resolving OCR inaccuracies
- Infrastructure Limitations: CLIP matching incomplete; usability constraints in validation tools

Artifacts Produced:

- OCR parsing scripts and extracted metadata outputs
- Enriched metadata mapping files
- Renamed crop image dataset
- Override logs and validation notes
- Visual matching test outputs

Status:

This phase concluded with a functional but partially constrained OCR and metadata enrichment pipeline. Core workflows—crop extraction, OCR parsing, and renaming—were established, with human-in-the-loop correction mechanisms ensuring data integrity.

Limitations in OCR accuracy and metadata mapping were identified, indicating the need for further refinement before fully automated catalog alignment can be relied upon.

Entry 31

Book Reference: Chapter 9
Date: 5 August 2025
Phase: Dataset Audit & Divergence Framework

Objective:

To harden the Monet dataset through quality auditing, deduplication, and patch extraction, and to design a multi-axis divergence-testing framework for future evaluation of Monet vs non-Monet separation.

Procedures Completed:

This phase focused on dataset quality control, structural preparation, and framework design. No similarity modeling or divergence testing was executed; only infrastructure and design development were performed.

A tiered quality audit was conducted across the full dataset to evaluate resolution, sharpness, dynamic range, compression artifacts, clipping, and patchability. Deduplication workflows were applied to remove exact and near-duplicate images, ensuring a balanced dataset.

Patch extraction pipelines were implemented to generate localized brushstroke samples, enabling future fine-grained modeling. Dataset tiering was introduced to separate high-confidence ("gold") images from usable ("silver") images.

In parallel, a divergence-testing framework was designed to support future evaluation across multiple analytical axes.

Dataset Hardening and Patch Infrastructure

Type	File / Script Examples	Nature of Work
Tiered Quality Audit	audit_tiered_patchability.py	Evaluated resolution, sharpness, dynamic range, artifacts
Patchability Testing	Audit outputs	Verified ≥150 usable 256×256 patches per image
Deduplication	dedupe_keep_best.py	Removed duplicate bias; retained highest-quality images
Tier Partitioning	TierA_gold/, TierB_silver/	Organized dataset by quality confidence
Patch Export	patch_exporter.py	Generated brushstroke-level training samples
Patch Indexing	_patches/ patch_index.csv	Structured patch-level dataset

Divergence Framework Design (Proposed)

Component	Description
Stroke Encoder	Contrastive model on Monet vs non-Monet patches
Style/Composition Encoder	Full-image embeddings (CLIP-like)
Multi-Axis Validator	Fusion of stroke, style, signature, and catalog signals
Evaluation Metrics	ROC AUC, PR AUC, Top-K ranking, component scoring
Additional Channels	FFT, wavelet, palette, signature, catalog alignment

Testing Conducted:

The following workflows were executed and validated:

- Full Dataset Audit: 7,892 images scanned across quality metrics
- Patchability Validation: Confirmed stroke-level ex tractability after mask logic correction
- Bug Fix (Mask Logic): Resolved false-negative patch scoring issue
- Deduplication: 6,211 duplicate images removed; highest-quality retained
- Tier Creation: Dataset partitioned into TierA_gold (359) and TierB_silver (96)
- Patch Export: Structured patch dataset successfully generated

Documented Outcomes

- Dataset Quality Stabilization: High-fidelity Monet corpus established
- Duplicate Bias Removed: Improved dataset balance and reliability
- Patch-Level Dataset Created: Enabled fine-grained stroke analysis
- Tiered Dataset Structure: Introduced quality-based dataset control
- Framework Defined: Multi-axis divergence system designed for future testing

Artifacts Produced:

- Tiered audit reports and quality metrics
- Deduplication logs and dataset reduction records
- Patch dataset exports and structured patch index
- TierA_gold and TierB_silver dataset folders

- Divergence framework design documentation

Status:

This phase concluded with a hardened Monet dataset and a fully defined divergence-testing framework. Dataset integrity, balance, and patch-level structure were established, providing a strong foundation for future similarity modeling and class-separation analysis.

Entry 32

Book Reference: Chapter 9
Date: 17 August 2025
Phase: Monet Quality Validation & Deep Filtering

Objective:

To validate and curate a high-quality Monet dataset by transitioning from heuristic-based filtering methods to deep-learning-based filtering using ResNet50 embeddings.

Procedures Completed:

This phase focused on dataset quality validation and filtering. No Study/Getty similarity testing or Monet vs non-Monet class-separation experiments were conducted.

Initial validation relied on heuristic filters, including sharpness, edge density, noise estimation, resolution thresholds, blockiness detection, and color entropy analysis. Multiple rounds of threshold tuning were performed to improve performance.

Due to consistent failure of heuristic filters to retain authentic Monet images, a deep-learning-based filtering approach was implemented. ResNet50 embeddings were extracted and compared via cosine similarity against a trusted Monet reference set. This method replaced heuristic filtering as the primary validation mechanism.

Dataset Validation Channels

Type	Script / File Examples	Nature of Work
Heuristic Quality Filter	validate_monet_image_quality.py	Rule-based filtering (focus, edges, noise, resolution)

Type	Script / File Examples	Nature of Work
Threshold Debugging	Revised scripts	Iterative tuning of Laplacian, Sobel, and noise thresholds
Pixelation Filter	Updated script	Detection of compression/block artifacts
Color Entropy Filter	Updated script	Detection of unnatural color distributions
Deep Learning Filter	deep_monet_filter.py	ResNet50 embedding similarity filtering

Testing Conducted:

Validation workflows were tested across multiple approaches:

- Heuristic Filtering (Initial): Rejected all 2,346 images due to mismatch with photographic assumptions
- Threshold Debugging: Partial improvement, but still failed to retain authentic Monet images
- Pixelation & Entropy Filters: Improved artifact detection but continued to reject valid works
- Deep Learning Filter (ResNet50): Successfully retained authentic Monet images while rejecting noisy or artificial inputs

Documented Outcomes

- Heuristic Failure: Rule-based filters proved incompatible with painterly image characteristics
- Threshold Instability: Iterative tuning did not resolve misclassification of valid Monet works
- Deep Filter Success: ResNet50 embeddings provided stable and reliable filtering

- Representation Shift: Transition from pixel-level heuristics to learned feature space
- Dataset Quality Improvement: High-quality Monet subset successfully established

Artifacts Produced:

- validate_monet_image_quality.py (multiple revisions)
- deep_monet_filter.py
- MonetProject2/high_quality_deep/ dataset
- deep_filter_scores.txt (cosine similarity logs)
- Image quality logs (heuristic and deep filtering results)

Status:

This phase concluded with a validated Monet dataset using deep embedding-based filtering. ResNet50 cosine similarity (threshold ≥ 0.85) was used to retain authentic Monet images and remove low-quality or synthetic inputs.

The transition from heuristic filtering to deep-learning-based validation was completed successfully, establishing a reliable dataset quality control mechanism for future modeling and analysis.

Entry 33

Book Reference: Chapter 9
Date: 17 August 2025
Phase: Duplicate Detection & Hash Testing

Objective:

To validate dataset integrity by refining duplicate detection methods and evaluating hash sensitivity across multiple perceptual hashing approaches.

Procedures Completed:

This phase focused on duplicate detection refinement and validation. No similarity modeling or divergence testing was conducted.

Multiple perceptual hashing methods (pHash, dHash, aHash) were applied to the Monet dataset. Sensitivity thresholds were systematically adjusted using Hamming distance tuning to evaluate detection behavior under varying conditions.

A multi-hash detection framework was implemented to improve robustness, combining multiple hash types with independent thresholds. Union-Find clustering was used to group potentially similar images, and quality-based selection logic was introduced to retain the highest-quality image within any detected group.

Special handling was implemented for Wildenstein-pattern filenames, ensuring that reference-aligned images were preserved unless clearly inferior. Hard deletion logic was included to remove duplicates where detected.

Duplicate Detection and Hash Sensitivity Testing

Type	Script / Method	Nature of Work
Initial Detection (pHash)	pHash (16)	Low-threshold duplicate detection (strict)
Threshold Adjustment	Hamming tuning	Increased sensitivity testing
Multi-Hash Detection	pHash, dHash, aHash	Combined hashing for robust detection
Clustering	Union-Find	Grouped potential duplicate candidates
Quality Selection	Resolution + sharpness weighting	Selected best image within groups
Wildenstein Handling	Filename rules	Preserved reference-aligned files
Deletion Logic	os.remove()	Permanent removal of detected duplicates

Testing Conducted:

Duplicate detection was evaluated across multiple configurations:

- Initial pHash detection (strict threshold): No duplicate groups detected
- Increased sensitivity thresholds: No duplicate groups detected
- Multi-hash detection (combined methods): No duplicate groups detected
- Quality-based selection logic validated (no groups triggered)

Documented Outcomes

- No Duplicate Groups Identified: Dataset showed no duplicate clusters across all tested methods
- Sensitivity Robustness: Detection remained stable under both strict and relaxed thresholds

- Multi-Hash Validation: Combined hashing confirmed absence of duplicate matches
- Dataset Integrity Confirmed: No redundancy detected within the evaluated dataset
- Pipeline Reliability: Detection framework validated for future use

Artifacts Produced:

- Refined duplicate detection scripts
- Hash sensitivity tuning documentation
- Duplicate detection logs (no matches detected)

Status:

This phase concluded with confirmation that no duplicate images were present under multiple perceptual hashing configurations. The duplicate detection pipeline was validated, and dataset integrity was confirmed for subsequent analysis.

Entry 34

Book Reference: Chapter 9
Date: 18 August 2025
Phase: Quality-Based File Management

Objective:

To operationalize duplicate detection within a file management framework, incorporating quality-based selection, deletion safeguards, and controlled dataset refinement.

Procedures Completed:

This phase extended duplicate detection into a full file management workflow. No similarity modeling or divergence testing was conducted.

Multi-hash duplicate detection methods (pHash, dHash, aHash) were applied with increased sensitivity thresholds. While no duplicate groups were identified, additional logic was implemented to support future detection scenarios.

A quality-based scoring system was introduced to rank images using resolution and sharpness metrics. This scoring system defined how duplicates would be resolved if detected, including weighted selection and tie-breaking rules.

Special handling was implemented for Wildenstein-pattern filenames to preserve reference-aligned images unless clearly inferior. File renaming safeguards were introduced to prevent overwriting or data loss during processing.

Hard deletion behavior was implemented with logging, ensuring that any detected duplicates would be permanently removed in a controlled and traceable manner.

Duplicate Detection and File Management Workflow

Type	Script / Method	Nature of Work
Multi-Hash Detection	pHash, dHash, aHash	High-sensitivity duplicate detection framework
Threshold Escalation	Hamming tuning	Expanded detection sensitivity
Quality Scoring	Resolution + sharpness weighting	Defined keeper selection logic
Wildenstein Rules	Filename-based handling	Preserved reference-aligned images
Renaming Safeguards	File handling logic	Prevented overwrite and data loss
Deletion Workflow	os.remove() + logs	Controlled and traceable removal process

Testing Conducted:

Duplicate detection and management workflows were evaluated:

- Multi-hash detection (high sensitivity): No duplicate groups identified
- Quality-based selection logic validated (no groups triggered)
- File renaming safeguards confirmed operational
- Hard deletion workflow verified (no deletions executed due to absence of duplicates)

Documented Outcomes

- No Duplicate Groups Identified: Consistent with prior validation

- Workflow Operationalization: Detection integrated with file management system
- Quality Selection Defined: Clear rules established for duplicate resolution
- Data Safety Ensured: Safeguards prevent accidental overwrite or loss
- Pipeline Readiness: System prepared for future duplicate handling scenarios

Artifacts Produced:

- Updated duplicate detection and file management scripts
- Quality scoring logic documentation
- Deletion logs (no duplicates removed)
- File management workflow documentation

Status:

This phase concluded with a fully operational duplicate detection and file management system. While no duplicates were identified, the workflow now includes quality-based selection, deletion controls, and safety mechanisms, ensuring readiness for future dataset refinement.

Entry 35

Book Reference: Chapter 9
Date: 31 August 2025
Phase: Interactive Matching Development

Objective:

To develop a human-in-the-loop workflow for matching Monet dataset images to Wildenstein references, while ensuring safe filename normalization, collision-resistant renaming, and organized dataset restructuring.

Procedures Completed:

This phase focused on building an interactive matching and renaming system. No similarity modeling or divergence testing was conducted.

Filename normalization workflows were implemented to standardize Wildenstein crop filenames, ensuring consistent matching behavior. Collision-safe renaming logic was introduced to prevent overwriting during filename truncation and transformation.

An interactive matching tool was developed using perceptual hashing to rank candidate matches. Human validation was integrated into the workflow, allowing manual confirmation prior to renaming. Visual contact sheets were generated to support side-by-side comparison between source images and top candidate matches.

User interaction flow was optimized through keyboard-driven controls, eliminating unnecessary input steps and improving workflow efficiency. Stability improvements were introduced to address external viewer issues and maintain terminal focus during interaction.

Accepted matches were renamed with extension preservation and relocated into a structured output directory to maintain dataset organization.

Interactive Matching and File Management Workflow

Type	Tool / Method	Nature of Work
Filename Normalization	truncate_wildenstein_filenames.py	Standardized filenames for reliable matching
Collision Handling	Suffix-based resolution	Prevented overwrite during truncation
Interactive Matching	match_and_rename.py (aHash + ranking)	Human-guided candidate selection
Visual Validation	Contact sheets (Top-5 previews)	Enabled side-by-side comparison
Input Optimization	Single-key controls	Streamlined interaction flow
Viewer Stability	Internal preview handling	Improved usability and focus control
Safe Renaming	Extension-preserving logic	Prevented data loss
File Relocation	MonetDataSet_Renamed/	Organized processed outputs

Testing Conducted:

Interactive workflow components were validated:

- Filename normalization confirmed consistent preprocessing
- Collision-safe renaming verified under truncation scenarios
- Perceptual hash ranking successfully generated candidate matches
- Contact-sheet previews validated for usability in manual selection

- Keyboard-driven interaction improved efficiency (no Enter required)
- Viewer stability improvements reduced focus interruptions
- File renaming preserved extensions and prevented overwrite
- Post-match relocation verified for clean dataset organization

Documented Outcomes

- Human-in-the-Loop Validation: Enabled controlled matching instead of automated renaming
- Workflow Efficiency: Optimized interaction through simplified input and preview systems
- Data Safety: Collision handling and rename safeguards prevented data loss
- Visual Verification: Contact sheets improved confidence in matching decisions
- Dataset Organization: Structured relocation of processed files

Artifacts Produced:

- Filename normalization scripts
- Interactive matching tool (match_and_rename.py)
- Contact-sheet preview generator
- Collision-safe renaming logic
- Organized output dataset (MonetDataSet_Renamed/)

Status:

This phase concluded with a fully operational interactive matching workflow. The system integrates human validation, safe renaming, and structured dataset organization, enabling reliable alignment between Monet dataset images and Wildenstein references.

Entry 36

Book Reference: Chapter 9
Date: 14 September 2025
Phase: Dataset Purification & Artifact Removal

Objective:

To purify the dataset by removing non-painting artifacts and ensure that all subsequent analytical phases operate exclusively on legitimate painting images.

Procedures Completed:

This phase implemented a systematic purification pipeline to eliminate non-painting materials, including OCR artifacts, catalog pages, margins, signatures, and thumbnails. No stylistic similarity, embedding analysis, or divergence testing was conducted.

A multi-stage filtering pipeline was applied using filename-based exclusion, geometric constraints, visual structure analysis, and content-based heuristics. The process was designed to remove non-painting artifacts while preserving images consistent with painted works.

The purification process was executed as a fully automated pipeline with hard deletion, supported by logging to ensure traceability and auditability.

Dataset Purification Pipeline

Type	Script / Method	Nature of Work
Keyword-Based Exclusion	purge_non_paintings.py	Removed files with non-painting indicators (e.g., "signature", "cover", "OCR")
File Size Gate	< 50 KB threshold	Eliminated thumbnails and

Type	Script / Method	Nature of Work
		low-content debris
Minimum Geometry	≥ 256 px dimension	Ensured sufficient structural area
Aspect Ratio Filtering	> 3.5:1 rejection	Removed margin strips and scan artifacts
Grayscale / Low Variance Detection	grayscale_and_variance_flags()	Filtered flat or text-like scans
Edge Density Analysis	edge_density()	Retained images with structural complexity
Hard Deletion Execution	Automated pipeline	Removed non-painting artifacts without manual review
Deletion Logging	_deleted_non_paintings.log	Recorded removal reasons for auditability

Testing Conducted:

The purification pipeline was executed end-to-end:

- All filtering stages applied sequentially via purge_non_paintings.py
- Non-painting artifacts successfully removed based on combined criteria
- Structural and visual thresholds verified across retained images
- Deletion logs confirmed traceability of all removed files

Documented Outcomes

- Artifact Removal: Non-painting elements (OCR debris, margins, thumbnails) eliminated
- Dataset Purification: Painting-only corpus established

- Structural Consistency: Retained images meet minimum visual and geometric criteria
- Automated Execution: Pipeline performed without manual intervention
- Auditability: Deletion logs provide full traceability

Artifacts Produced:

- purge_non_paintings.py
- _deleted_non_paintings.log
- Cleaned painting-only dataset

Status:

This phase concluded with a purified dataset containing only painting images. The corpus is now free of non-painting artifacts and is suitable for subsequent modeling, similarity analysis, and divergence testing.

Entry 37

Book Reference: Chapter 9
Date: 21 September 2025
Phase: Automated Painting-Only Purification

Objective:

To validate the stability and repeatability of the automated dataset purification pipeline, ensuring that rule-based filtering consistently produces a painting-only dataset.

Procedures Completed:

This phase re-executed and validated the rule-based purification pipeline previously established. No stylistic analysis, embedding evaluation, or divergence testing was conducted.

The same multi-stage filtering system was applied, including keyword-based exclusion, geometric thresholds, structural analysis, and content-based heuristics. The objective was to confirm that the purification logic performs consistently across runs and does not introduce unintended data loss or retention errors.

Deletion logging was maintained to verify traceability and confirm that removal criteria were applied consistently.

Purification Validation Pipeline

Type	Method	Validation Focus
Keyword Filtering	Filename-based rules	Consistency of non-painting exclusion
File Size Gate	< 50 KB threshold	Stability of artifact removal
Geometry Filtering	≥ 256 px constraint	Structural consistency of retained images

Type	Method	Validation Focus
Aspect Ratio Filtering	> 3.5:1 rejection	Repeatability of scan artifact removal
Variance Detection	Grayscale / low variance	Reliability of content-based filtering
Edge Density Analysis	Structural gradients	Consistency of visual complexity filtering
Hard Delete Execution	Automated pipeline	Repeatability of removal decisions
Deletion Logging	Audit logs	Verification of deterministic behavior

Testing Conducted:

The purification pipeline was re-executed to confirm stability:

- All filtering stages produced consistent results with prior execution
- No unexpected retention of non-painting artifacts observed
- No excessive removal of valid painting images detected
- Deletion logs confirmed repeatability of filtering decisions

Documented Outcomes

- Pipeline Stability: Filtering behavior consistent across executions
- Repeatability Confirmed: Same criteria produced consistent dataset outputs
- No Regression Observed: No reintroduction of non-painting artifacts
- Dataset Integrity Maintained: Painting-only corpus preserved

Artifacts Produced:

- Updated purification scripts (validated)
- Deletion logs confirming repeatability
- Verified painting-only dataset

Status:

This phase confirmed that the rule-based purification pipeline is stable and repeatable. The painting-only dataset has been validated across multiple executions, ensuring consistent preparation for downstream modeling and analysis.

Entry 38

Book Reference: Chapter 9
Date: 28 September 2025
Phase: Openverse API Troubleshooting

Objective:

To attempt automated acquisition of Monet images from the Openverse platform and diagnose barriers to API-based dataset retrieval.

Procedures Completed:

This phase focused on external dataset acquisition attempts and troubleshooting. No similarity modeling, embedding analysis, or divergence testing was conducted.

API-based retrieval workflows were implemented to query the Openverse public API for Monet images. When access failures occurred, fallback strategies were tested, including HTML-based scraping and script-level adjustments to request handling.

Network diagnostics were performed to isolate potential connectivity issues. Multiple iterations of the retrieval script were developed to test authentication handling, headers, redirects, and endpoint variations.

Dataset Acquisition and Troubleshooting

Type	Script / Method	Nature of Work
API Querying	openverse_monet_scraper.py	Attempted automated retrieval via Openverse API
Authentication Handling	Script revisions	Tested headers, tokens, and request formats
HTML Scraping	Revised scraper	Attempted frontend

Type	Script / Method	Nature of Work
Fallback		extraction of image URLs
Network Diagnostics	curl / TLS inspection	Verified connectivity, DNS, and redirects
Compatibility Iterations	Multiple script versions	Explored alternate request configurations

Testing Conducted:

Acquisition and troubleshooting workflows were evaluated:

- API Retrieval Attempt: Returned 401 Unauthorized error
- HTML Scraping Attempt: Failed due to JavaScript-rendered content
- Network Verification: Confirmed no connectivity or DNS issues
- Script Iterations: Tested header injection, redirects, and endpoint variations without success

Documented Outcomes

- API Access Restriction: Openverse API requests blocked by authorization requirements
- Scraping Limitation: Frontend content not directly accessible via static HTML parsing
- Network Integrity: Local environment verified as non-causal
- Failure Isolation: Issue attributed to API access constraints, not implementation error

Artifacts Produced:

- openverse_monet_scraper.py (multiple revisions)
- Network diagnostic notes

- API troubleshooting documentation

Status:

This phase concluded with unsuccessful dataset acquisition due to API authorization restrictions. The failure was isolated to external access constraints rather than script or network issues.

No dataset was acquired, and no analytical workflows were executed. The results indicate that alternative acquisition strategies are required for Openverse-based data retrieval.

Entry 39

Book Reference: Chapter 9
Date: 30 September 2025
Phase: Interactive Matching & UI Validation

Objective:

To validate and refine an interactive, high-performance matching system for aligning Monet reference images with Wildenstein catalog datasets, emphasizing usability, speed, and reliable renaming.

Procedures Completed:

This phase focused on optimizing and validating an interactive matching workflow. No similarity modeling or divergence testing was conducted.

A human-in-the-loop matching system was refined to support rapid visual comparison between query images and Wildenstein reference datasets (Volumes VII and VIII). The system was designed for efficient navigation, reliable candidate selection, and safe renaming based on authoritative reference identifiers.

Performance and usability improvements were introduced, including optimized hashing for candidate retrieval, UI scaling for high-resolution displays, and streamlined interaction controls. Ambiguities in filename parsing were identified and resolved by replacing inference logic with direct reuse of reference identifiers.

Interactive Matching and UI Validation

Type	Tool / Method	Nature of Work
Interactive Matching	matcher.py	Human-guided selection across query and

Type	Tool / Method	Nature of Work
		candidate sets
Perceptual Hash Indexing	pHash-based retrieval	Fast candidate ranking and paging
UI Scaling	4K grid layout	Simultaneous display of 10 candidates without clipping
Filename Parsing	Regex attempt (VII/VIII)	Identified ambiguity in substring matching
Canonical Renaming	Reference ID reuse	Eliminated mislabeling risk
Duplicate Handling	Suffix-based naming	Prevented overwrite during collisions
Performance Optimization	pHash vs multi-hash	Restored responsiveness by reverting to pHash

Testing Conducted:

Workflow performance and usability were evaluated:

- Interactive matching validated with human-in-the-loop selection (1–10, navigation, skip)
- Candidate retrieval confirmed fast and responsive under pHash indexing
- UI layout validated for full visibility on high-resolution displays
- Filename parsing tested; ambiguity identified and corrected
- Canonical renaming verified using reference identifiers
- Duplicate handling confirmed via collision-safe naming

- Performance regression identified with multi-hash approach; resolved by reverting to pHash

Documented Outcomes

- Workflow Maturity: Stable and efficient interactive matching system established
- Performance Optimization: Fast candidate retrieval and responsive UI achieved
- Usability Improvements: Clear visual comparison and simplified interaction flow
- Renaming Reliability: Reference-based naming eliminated ambiguity
- Collision Safety: Duplicate handling prevents data loss
- System Refinement: Inefficient multi-hash approach replaced with performance alternative

Artifacts Produced:

- matcher.py (multiple iterations)
- Curated Monet image archive (~1,176 images)
- Wildenstein VII & VIII alignment mappings
- Catalog cross-verification notes
- Revalidated non-Monet control reference set

Status:

This phase concluded with a validated interactive matching and alignment system. The workflow supports efficient human-guided matching, reliable renaming, and high-performance candidate retrieval, providing a stable foundation for dataset authentication and subsequent analytical testing.

Entry 40

Book Reference: Chapter 9
Date: 01 October 2025 – 23 December 2025
Phase: Monet Images & Catalog Validation

Objective:

To authenticate the Monet dataset by verifying collected images against the Wildenstein catalog and establish a high-confidence, catalog-aligned reference corpus for subsequent analytical testing.

Procedures Completed:

This phase integrated automated matching, interactive validation, and manual catalog verification to authenticate the Monet dataset.

An initial corpus of over 1,176 Monet images was assembled from multiple sources. Automated matching approaches (including perceptual hashing and ranking methods) were applied to align images with Wildenstein catalog references. Due to limitations in automated accuracy, a human-in-the-loop workflow was used to validate candidate matches.

Final confirmation was performed through direct comparison with Wildenstein catalog volumes (VII and VIII). Only images that could be confidently matched to catalog entries were retained. The dataset was strictly filtered to ensure alignment with authoritative catalog records.

The non-Monet control dataset was revalidated in parallel to ensure integrity for future comparative analysis.

Dataset Authentication and Validation Workflow

Type	Method	Nature of Work
Initial Dataset Assembly	Multi-source collection	Compiled >1,176 Monet images
Automated Matching	pHash, ORB, ranking methods	Generated candidate alignments
Interactive Validation	Human-in-the-loop matcher	Confirmed matches visually
Manual Catalog Verification	Wildenstein volumes VII & VIII	Final authoritative confirmation
Catalog-Constrained Filtering	Reference alignment	Retained only verifiable works
Control Set Revalidation	non-Monet dataset review	Ensured integrity of comparison set

Testing Conducted:

Validation workflows were applied across the dataset:

- Automated matching used to generate candidate alignments
- Interactive matching validated candidate selections through visual inspection
- Manual catalog verification confirmed alignment with authoritative references
- Ambiguities resolved through direct catalog comparison
- Dataset consistency verified after filtering

Documented Outcomes

- Dataset Reduction: >1,176 images reduced to 786 verified Monet works
- Ground-Truth Established: All retained images aligned with Wildenstein catalog entries

- Hybrid Validation Approach: Automation supported by human and manual verification
- Error Mitigation: Automated misalignments corrected through manual confirmation
- Control Integrity: non-Monet reference set revalidated

Artifacts Produced:

- Curated Monet image archive (>1,176 initial images)
- Matcher system iterations and validation workflow
- Wildenstein VII & VIII alignment mappings
- Catalog cross-verification documentation
- Final authenticated dataset (786 confirmed works)
- Revalidated non-Monet control dataset

Status:

This phase concluded with the creation of a high-confidence, Wildenstein-verified Monet dataset. The corpus was reduced from over 1,176 collected images to 786 authenticated works, each aligned with catalog references.

This dataset serves as the ground-truth reference for all subsequent analytical, embedding-based, and divergence testing phases.

Entry 41

Book Reference: Chapter 9
Date: 24 December 2025
Phase: Image Matching System Evaluation

Objective:

To refine and performance-optimize the interactive image-matching system following dataset authentication, ensuring efficient operation, accurate alignment, and reliable file handling for future use.

Procedures Completed:

This phase focused on system-level refinement and performance evaluation of the interactive matching workflow. No dataset expansion or new authentication was conducted.

Following the completion of dataset authentication, the matching system was further optimized to improve speed, usability, and reliability. Multiple matching approaches—including ORB feature matching, perceptual hashing, and hybrid ranking methods—were evaluated to balance accuracy and responsiveness.

GPU availability and utilization were verified to ensure compatibility with computational workloads. Performance tradeoffs between fast perceptual methods and more computationally intensive feature-based approaches were analyzed.

System reliability improvements included canonical renaming enforcement and duplicate collision handling, ensuring safe file operations during matching workflows.

Matching System Refinement and Performance Evaluation

Type	Method	Nature of Work
ORB Feature Matching	OpenCV ORB	Evaluated keypoint-based alignment accuracy
Perceptual Hash Matching	pHash baseline	Optimized fast global similarity ranking
Multi-Method Ranking	Hybrid approaches	Tested accuracy vs latency tradeoffs
GPU Verification	nvidia-smi	Confirmed RTX 4090 availability and utilization
Performance Testing	Paging latency (N/S navigation)	Compared responsiveness across methods
Interactive Review Workflow	Query + 10 candidate grid	Validated efficient human-in-the-loop matching
Canonical Renaming	Reference ID reuse	Ensured consistent and accurate file naming
Duplicate Handling	Suffix logic (_dupe, _1, _2)	Prevented overwrite during collisions

Testing Conducted:

System performance and reliability were evaluated:

- ORB matching tested for structural alignment capability
- pHash confirmed as fastest method for candidate retrieval
- Hybrid methods evaluated but introduced latency tradeoffs
- GPU availability verified, though not required for all workflows
- Interactive workflow validated for speed and usability
- Renaming logic confirmed to prevent mislabeling
- Duplicate handling validated under collision scenarios

Documented Outcomes

- Performance Optimization: pHash retained as primary method due to speed
- Accuracy Tradeoffs: ORB and hybrid methods improved detail but reduced responsiveness
- System Stability: Matching workflow operates reliably under repeated use
- Safe File Handling: Renaming and collision logic prevent data loss
- GPU Readiness: System compatible with accelerated environments

Artifacts Produced:

- Refined matcher.py (multiple optimized versions)
- Performance benchmarking notes (pHash vs ORB vs hybrid)
- Updated alignment mappings (Wildenstein VII & VIII)
- Workflow documentation for optimized matching system
- Revalidated non-Monet control dataset logs

Status:

This phase concluded with a refined and performance-optimized matching system. The workflow balances speed, usability, and accuracy, with pHash-based retrieval serving as the primary method and more complex approaches reserved for targeted validation scenarios.

The system is stable, efficient, and ready to support subsequent analytical and modeling phases.

Entry 42

Book Reference: Chapter 10
Date: 26 December 2025
Phase: Model Strategy & Dataset Planning

Objective:

To define modeling strategies and prepare the authenticated Monet dataset for embedding-based analysis, classification, and metric-learning workflows.

Procedures Completed:

This phase focused on conceptual modeling design and dataset structuring. Limited exploratory testing was conducted to validate feasibility. No full-scale model training or final evaluation was performed.

The authenticated Monet dataset (644 works) was evaluated alongside a broader multi-artist dataset (~50 artists; ~8,000 total images). Multiple modeling approaches were defined, including embedding-based retrieval, binary classification, multi-class classification, and metric-learning strategies.

Dataset composition, class balance, and data-splitting strategies were developed to ensure proper training conditions and prevent data leakage. Particular emphasis was placed on including stylistically similar "hard negatives" (e.g., Impressionist painters) to strengthen model discrimination.

Proposed Modeling and Embedding Strategies

Type	Method	Purpose
CLIP Embedding Indexing	CLIP + cosine similarity	Evaluate stylistic proximity via nearest-neighbor search

Type	Method	Purpose
Similarity Distribution Testing	Monet-to-Monet baseline	Define “in-family” similarity thresholds
Binary Classification	Monet vs non-Monet	Test separability of Monet works
Multi-Class Classification	~50 artist classifier	Evaluate broader artist-level discrimination
Metric Learning	Contrastive / Triplet networks	Learn embedding space with clustered Monet representations
Dataset Composition	Hard negative inclusion	Prevent confusion with stylistically similar artists
Data Splitting Strategy	Group-aware partitioning	Prevent leakage across training/validation/test sets

Testing Conducted (Exploratory):

Initial feasibility checks were performed:

- CLIP embeddings evaluated for intra-Monet similarity consistency
- Monet similarity distribution examined to estimate baseline thresholds
- Binary classification tested for basic separability (Monet vs non-Monet)
- Multi-class classification feasibility explored across ~50 artists
- Metric-learning approach (Triplet) tested at a preliminary level
- Dataset composition reviewed to ensure inclusion of hard negatives
- Data-splitting strategies validated to prevent leakage

Documented Outcomes

- Strategy Definition: Multiple viable modeling paths established
- Dataset Readiness: 644 Monet works integrated into structured dataset (~8,000 images total)
- Feasibility Confirmed: Embedding, classification, and metric-learning approaches all viable
- Evaluation Framework: Defined similarity thresholds, classification metrics, and validation structure
- Leakage Prevention: Group-aware splitting strategy established

Artifacts Produced:

- Modeling strategy documentation
- Dataset structure and composition plan
- Preliminary embedding and similarity analysis outputs
- Data-splitting and leakage prevention guidelines

Status:

This phase concluded with a defined modeling strategy and a prepared dataset for machine learning workflows. The groundwork for embedding analysis, classification, and metric learning has been established, with exploratory testing confirming feasibility.

Subsequent phases will focus on full model implementation, training, and evaluation.

Entry 43

Book Reference: Chapter 10
Date: 28 December 2025
Phase: Testing Restart & Method Clarification

Objective:

To reset the analytical framework, eliminate ambiguity from prior testing phases, and establish a standardized structure for reporting similarity and divergence results.

Procedures Completed:

This phase formalized the methodological foundation for all subsequent analytical work. No similarity modeling, embedding evaluation, or divergence testing was conducted.

The testing process was intentionally reset to ensure consistency and clarity moving forward. A structured reporting framework was introduced, separating all future results into two distinct categories:

- **Non-Separation** (similarity / alignment)
- **Separation** (divergence / distinction)

This distinction was defined to prevent ambiguity in interpretation and to ensure that similarity findings and divergence findings are explicitly separated in all future documentation.

A standardized reporting format was established and applied as the required structure for all subsequent entries.

Framework Standardization

Type	Method	Purpose
Testing Reset	Project re-	Removed ambiguity from

Type	Method	Purpose
	initialization	prior phases
Methodological Clarification	Structured framework definition	Defined separation of similarity vs divergence
Reporting Standardization	Two-section format	Ensured consistent documentation across entries

Testing Conducted (Framework Validation):

The framework was validated through structural checks:

- Testing reset confirmed as complete and clearly documented
- Non-Separation vs Separation distinction defined and unambiguous
- Reporting format validated for consistency and repeatability
- Documentation structure confirmed for future analytical phases

Documented Outcomes

- Framework Reset: Analytical process re-initialized with clear structure
- Conceptual Clarity: Explicit separation between similarity and divergence
- Documentation Consistency: Standardized format established for all future entries
- Interpretation Control: Reduced risk of ambiguity in analytical conclusions

Artifacts Produced:

- Framework definition documentation (Markdown)
- Standardized reporting template

- Testing reset documentation

Status:

This phase concluded with a fully defined analytical framework. All subsequent testing and analysis will follow the standardized two-section structure (Non-Separation vs Separation), ensuring clarity, consistency, and interpretability of results.

Part III

Hardened Structural Testing

CHAPTER 10

Hardened Surface-Level Testing

As the inquiry neared completion, hardened surface-level testing became the focus of final validation. By this point, execution procedures had been fixed, and interpretive boundaries were established. What remained was a final stress test. The stabilized system was used to retest behavior across the entire set of Study Images, reference material, and non-reference comparisons, under conditions designed to reveal any remaining dependence on fragile structure or hidden influences.

What follows is one of the final surface-level tests conducted within the fixed environment and the defined scope of the inquiry. Its purpose was to confirm three key points:

1. That the same locked procedure could be restarted cleanly and executed again.
2. That scale and edge-case checks could be introduced without altering the procedure.
3. That it could do both without straying from the intended process, changing behavior under pressure, or producing patterns beyond what the approach could reliably support.

Stress-Testing Under Fully Fixed Rules

In this phase, the testing process remained unchanged. The framework was considered complete and subjected to deliberately challenging conditions to see if earlier behavior would hold, weaken, or change.

Under these conditions, the inquiry entered a phase of intense testing. Everything was done according to strict rules, with very little room for changes. Stress testing, in this case, meant running the process through controlled checks, while keeping the testing steps the same.

Brushwork-Isolation Transforms

Brushwork-isolation transforms were applied one at a time. Each pass altered only a single transformation so that its effect could be directly observed under the same fixed procedure. A "transform" refers to a controlled change applied to the image, such as converting to grayscale, normalizing contrast, dividing into patches, or filtering to emphasize texture over composition.

The goal was to remove more immediate visual cues, like color and overall scene layout, and see if the same proximity pattern held. The sequence followed a deliberate order:

- The images were converted to grayscale, and the contrast was adjusted to reduce the impact of lighting differences.
- Small random patches were taken from the images to focus less on the overall picture.
- Filters were used to reduce blur and broad shading, while bringing out sharper details like edges and fine textures.
- Filters were applied to reduce digital noise while keeping the edges clear.

Explicit "hard negatives" were introduced as a challenge by adding a small group of non-Monet images that resembled Monet in style and time period. The goal was to see if Monet references would still be the closest matches when these similar images were included. These images were selected from painters with similar styles and periods.

The model's core settings were locked, remaining the same throughout the testing. The list of Monet reference images used in each test was fixed, and the model wasn't retrained or adjusted during the analysis. The Study Images were kept completely separate from the training process, preventing any influence from the model itself.

Recording Stability Under Stress

When the Study Images remained near Monet references and separate from non-Monet material during these transformations, that consistency was recorded as procedural stability under stress, with interpretation confined to the limits of the testing procedure.

Artificial intelligence helped by running checks, comparing results, and writing descriptions of what the system produced. During this process, it identified a recurring risk in this kind of work. One of the techniques used for analyzing images is called PCA (Principal Component Analysis), which helps reduce the complexity of the data while keeping the key features intact. Although PCA is often seen as a harmless tool used to visualize patterns, it still learns patterns from the data it's given.

The issue arises when PCA is applied to the entire dataset, including the test images. In that case, it can accidentally pull in information from the test images, affecting the results. To avoid this, the test images were kept separate from the rest of the data, and the process was set up to prevent mixing everything together. When the AI suggested any conclusions beyond the data it had, that pressure was carefully monitored and kept under control.

AI Collaboration
Keeping test folds isolated: Dismissed.

AI Output
If PCA is applied to the full dataset, the test folds have influenced the transform.

Author's Note
The steps in the process were kept the same to avoid errors and inconsistencies. The model was not adjusted based on the entire dataset.

Revalidation as an Independence Check

With stress testing complete, the inquiry moved into revalidation to confirm independence from continuity, familiarity, and execution history. Since the framework appeared stable, it should be able to exhibit the same behavior when tested again under the same conditions.

Revalidation proceeded under a clean execution context. Scripts were regenerated to restate the logic, without revision. Manifests were reloaded from scratch. Embeddings were recomputed from the beginning.

Artificial intelligence participated throughout revalidation, assisting with execution and descriptions of what appeared. Its interpretive impulses were allowed to surface, but decisive judgment remained human.

AI Collaboration
Interpretative escalation: Excluded.

AI Output
Revalidation may confirm robustness and strengthen confidence in earlier findings.

Author's Note
Revalidation was conducted to expose contradictions, should they appear, when the framework was re-entered without reliance on procedural familiarity.

Under revalidation, the framework behaved as it had before. The Study Images again occupied overlapping neighborhoods with Monet reference material while remaining distinct from the broader non-Monet comparison set. As the images underwent changes through gradually destructive transforms, the similarity between the images decreased as was expected, but then recovered and returned to the same pattern that was observed before the hardened changes began.

What This Phase Established

This chapter showed that the analytical framework held its shape under tightened control, stress conditions, and revalidation passes. Stability here meant that the framework behaved consistently when the execution terms were fixed, the process was repeated from the beginning, and the same overall pattern of similarity continued to appear.

By this stage, the inquiry had reached its intended ending: the point at which the original question had been answered, and continuing further would begin to change what was being tested by narrowing the data, restricting variation, or removing features this analysis was meant to observe.

With the analytical scope satisfied, this work was considered complete. The inquiry then turns to two narrowly bounded edge cases within the fixed framework, with stability treated as established. The next chapter addresses support-level weave behavior. The following chapter returns to the signature under the hardened procedure.

Entries 44-48

Entry 44

Book Reference: Chapter 10
Date: 30 December 2025
Phase: DINOv2 Geometry & k-NN Testing

Section 1: Non-Separation in Feature Distributions

Objective:

To evaluate whether Study tiles occupy the same feature-space region as Monet works using DINOv2 embeddings under controlled (Monet-only) and competitive conditions.

Procedures Completed:

Standardized 512×512 crops were generated across Study, Monet, and non-Monet datasets using identical tiling rules to ensure geometric comparability.

DINOv2 (ViT-L/14) embeddings were extracted (1024-D, L2-normalized), providing an unsupervised representation of image structure.

A Monet internal baseline was established using leave-one-painting-out (LOPO) nearest-neighbor distances to define expected intra-Monet variation.

k-NN testing was performed under:

- Monet-only conditions (control)
- Competitive conditions (Monet + non-Monet gallery)

Getty images were excluded from this phase.

Non-Separation Channels

Type	Method	Purpose
Standardized Cropping	make_crops.py	Eliminated sampling bias across datasets
De-Duplication	Stem-based filtering	Prevented artificial clustering
DINOv2 Embeddings	ViT-L/14	Generated geometric feature representations
Monet Baseline	LOPO distances	Defined intra-Monet variation
Monet-Only k-NN	Study vs Monet	Control condition
Competitive k-NN	Monet + non-Monet	Stress-test manifold membership
Distance Testing	Median comparisons	Geometry-based validation
Export Robustness	JPEG Save vs Export	Ruled out compression artifacts
Stability Audit	knn_confirm.py	Verified per-tile consistency

Documented Outcomes (Non-Separation)

- Monet-only testing: Study tiles achieved Monet-vote@10 = 1.000
- Competitive k-NN: Study tiles retained ~0.89 Monet vote dominance
- Stability: Results consistent across tiles; variation tied to crop content
- Robustness: Export method and compression did not affect outcomes

Section 2: Divergence in Feature Distributions

Objective:

To measure geometric separation between Monet and non-Monet works and evaluate Study placement relative to both distributions.

Separation Channels

Type	Measurement	Interpretation
Distance Geometry	Study → Monet = 0.253	Closer to Monet
Distance Geometry	Study → non-Monet = 0.310	Further from non-Monet
k-NN Stability	Threshold framework	Defined interpretation bands
Competitive Voting	~0.89 Monet	Monet-dominant under competition

Documented Outcomes (Separation)

- Study tiles are closer to Monet than to non-Monet in embedding space
- Competitive voting confirms Monet-dominant alignment
- Separation between Monet and non-Monet distributions is measurable
- Variability driven by crop selection, not processing artifacts

Summary of This Phase

This phase applied DINOv2 embeddings and k-NN testing to evaluate feature-space relationships between Study, Monet, and non-Monet datasets.

Under control conditions, Study tiles aligned fully with Monet neighbors. Under competitive conditions, Monet remained the dominant nearest-neighbor class, though not exclusively.

Distance-based analysis confirmed that Study tiles are positioned closer to Monet than to non-Monet works, while still reflecting natural intra-dataset variation.

Conclusion

DINOv2-based manifold analysis demonstrates that Study tiles exhibit strong geometric proximity to Monet works in feature space.

Competitive testing confirms that this proximity persists when non-Monet works are introduced, though with reduced dominance.

These results indicate consistent non-separation from Monet and measurable separation from non-Monet, while remaining sensitive to crop-level variability.

Entry 45

Book Reference: Chapter 10
Date: 30 December 2025
Phase: Embedding Stability & Adversarial Controls

Section 1: Non-Separation in Feature Distributions

Objective:

To evaluate whether Study images maintain stable geometric proximity to Monet under adversarial conditions and statistical validation, and to determine whether observed similarity exceeds chance-level behavior.

Procedures Completed:

Standardized 512×512 crops were generated and embedded using DINOv2 (1024-D feature space).

Robustness testing was conducted across multiple dimensions:

- duplicate control
- metric variation
- export pathway validation
- cross-source validation
- statistical significance testing

Getty images remained excluded.

Non-Separation Channels

Type	Method	Purpose
Crop Standardization	make_crops.py	Removed framing/resolution bias

Type	Method	Purpose
De-Duplication	Stem filtering	Prevented artificial clustering
Embedding Extraction	DINOv2	Generated geometric feature space
Distance CDF Analysis	CDF plots	Compared distribution overlap
k-NN Stability	k ∈ {1–50}	Tested robustness across parameters
Competitive k-NN	Monet + non-Monet	Stress-tested alignment
LOPO Validation	Leave-one-painting-out	Prevented source leakage
Permutation Test	Label randomization	Tested against null hypothesis
Metric Robustness	Cosine / L2 / Mahalanobis	Verified metric independence
Artist-Stratified Controls	Per-artist comparison	Prevented single-artist bias
ROC Calibration	Threshold analysis	Quantified classification tradeoffs
Export Controls	Save vs Export	Eliminated compression artifacts

Documented Outcomes (Non-Separation)

- Study images consistently cluster near Monet across embedding conditions
- Competitive k-NN: Monet dominance ≈ 0.97 (k ≥ 5)
- k-NN stability maintained across parameter range (no tuning bias)
- Metric robustness confirmed across distance measures

- LOPO validation shows consistency under cross-source exclusion
- Permutation testing rejects chance-level explanation ($p \approx 0.001$)
- Export and preprocessing artifacts ruled out

Section 2: Divergence in Feature Distributions

Objective:

To quantify separation between Monet and non-Monet feature spaces and evaluate Study placement relative to both distributions.

Separation Channels

Type	Measurement	Interpretation
Distance Geometry	Monet → Monet ≈ 0.105	Tight internal manifold
Distance Geometry	Study → Monet ≈ 0.253	Near Monet distribution
Distance Geometry	Study → non-Monet ≈ 0.310	Further from non-Monet
Competitive k-NN	≈ 0.97 Monet	Strong class dominance
Permutation Test	AUC ≈ 0.79; p ≈ 0.001	Statistically significant separation
LOPO Validation	Mean AUC ≈ 0.79	Cross-source stability

Documented Outcomes (Separation)

- Study images are closer to Monet than to non-Monet in embedding space
- Monet vs non-Monet separation is statistically significant
- Separation persists under adversarial controls (LOPO, permutation)

- No evidence that results are driven by duplication, bias, or preprocessing artifacts

Summary of This Phase

This phase extended prior manifold analysis by introducing adversarial controls and statistical validation.

Embedding behavior was tested under multiple constraints, including parameter variation, cross-source exclusion, and randomized baselines.

Across all conditions, Study images remained consistently closer to Monet than to non-Monet, while Monet and non-Monet distributions remained separable.

Conclusion

Embedding robustness testing demonstrates that the Study–Monet proximity observed in prior phases is stable, reproducible, and statistically significant.

Adversarial controls confirm that this proximity is not attributable to:

- duplication
- preprocessing artifacts
- parameter selection
- dataset bias

The results support a consistent pattern of non-separation from Monet and measurable separation from non-Monet, while remaining sensitive to natural variation within the dataset.

Entry 46

Book Reference: Chapter 10
Date: 31 December 2025
Phase: Hardening Brushstroke-level Analysis

Section 1: Non-Separation in Feature Distributions

Objective:

To refine and stabilize brushstroke-level feature extraction, ensuring consistent and reliable structural comparison between Study and Monet images without introducing instability into prior results.

Procedures Completed:

This phase focused on strengthening the brushstroke-level analysis pipeline. No new similarity testing or divergence analysis was conducted.

Pipeline refinements were applied to improve extraction of stroke orientation, directional structure, and micro-textural features from standardized image tiles. Implementation issues were corrected to eliminate potential artifacts in feature computation.

Stability checks were performed to verify that modifications to the pipeline did not alter previously observed similarity relationships.

Non-Separation Channels

Type	Method	Purpose
Brushstroke Pipeline Hardening	MonetProject7 scripts	Reduced noise and improved feature consistency
Stroke Feature Extraction	Orientation & texture outputs	Captured directional and micro-structural information

Type	Method	Purpose
Stability Validation	Re-run checks	Confirmed no drift in prior results
Cross-Crop Consistency	Tile-based comparisons	Ensured uniform feature behavior across regions
Implementation Fixes	Script corrections	Removed computational artifacts

Documented Outcomes (Non-Separation)

- Brushstroke feature extraction stabilized across pipeline refinements
- No change observed in prior similarity relationships after reprocessing
- Feature consistency maintained across crops and tiles
- Implementation artifacts eliminated

Section 2: Divergence in Feature Distributions

No Study/Monet vs non-Monet divergence testing was conducted during this phase.

Summary of This Phase

This phase focused on strengthening the reliability of brushstroke-level feature extraction rather than producing new analytical results.

Pipeline refinements were validated through stability checks, confirming that prior embedding and similarity findings remain unchanged under improved feature extraction conditions.

Conclusion

Brushstroke-level pipeline hardening improved the consistency and reliability of structural feature extraction without altering prior analytical outcomes.

These refinements reinforce confidence in earlier similarity and embedding results by demonstrating that they are stable under improved feature-processing conditions.

Entry 47

Book Reference: Chapter 10
Date: 01 January 2026
Phase: Brushwork & Patch-Level Validation

Section 1: Non-Separation in Feature Distributions

Objective:

To evaluate whether Study–Monet proximity persists when global composition, color, and low-frequency structure are removed, isolating local brushwork and micro-structural features.

Procedures Completed:

This phase introduced adversarial transformations to isolate local structure and test whether similarity signals remain stable under degraded or partial representations.

Transformations applied:

- grayscale + local contrast normalization (LCN)
- patch-level cropping (224×224)
- high-pass filtering (Laplacian)
- deterministic patch sampling

All embeddings were generated using DINOv2 (ViT-L/14, 1024-D).

Getty images remained excluded.

Non-Separation Channels

Type	Method	Purpose
Baseline Embedding	run_embeddings.py	Established pre-transform similarity
Grayscale + LCN	gray_lcn transform	Removed color and tonal bias
Patch Cropping	224×224 tiles	Isolated local brushwork
High-Pass Filtering	Laplacian	Removed low-frequency composition
Deterministic Sampling	Seeded patch selection	Prevented sampling bias
Large-Scale Embedding	269,950 patches	Enabled statistical comparison
kNN Margin Analysis	Monet vs non-Monet	Evaluated patch-level dominance
LOPO Validation	Cross-source testing	Prevented leakage
Permutation Testing	Label randomization	Tested against chance baseline

Quantitative Evidence

Metric	Value	Interpretation
Total Patches	269,950	Full dataset scale
Study Patches	160	Patch sample size
Monet Patches	18,840	Reference manifold
non-Monet Patches	250,950	Competitive set
Monet Top-1	49 / 160	Monet strongest match in ~31%
Monet Top-25	140 / 160	Monet appears in

Metric	Value	Interpretation
		~87.5%
Mean Similarity	0.7627	High structural similarity
Mean Margin	−0.00734	Monet slightly closer than non-Monet

Documented Outcomes (Non-Separation)

• Study patches retrieve Monet neighbors under all transformations
• Similarity persists after removal of color and composition
• Patch-level behavior distributed across image (not localized)
• kNN dominance remains high (~97% at $k \geq 5$, full-image context)
• LOPO validation confirms cross-source consistency (AUC ≈ 0.79)
• Permutation testing rejects random alignment ($p \approx 0.001$)

Section 2: Divergence in Feature Distributions

Objective:

To evaluate whether Study images remain closer to Monet than non-Monet under patch-level and adversarial conditions.

Separation Channels

Type	Measurement	Interpretation
Distance Geometry	Study → Monet < Study → non-Monet	Relative proximity maintained
kNN Separation	Monet-dominant	Stable class preference

Type	Measurement	Interpretation
	voting	
Permutation Test	AUC ≈ 0.79; p ≈ 0.001	Non-random separation
LOPO Validation	Cross-source AUC ≈ 0.79	Generalizable separation

Documented Outcomes (Separation)

- Study images remain closer to Monet than to non-Monet
- Separation is statistically significant
- Results persist under patch-level degradation
- No collapse observed under adversarial conditions

Summary of This Phase

This phase tested whether similarity signals persist when images are reduced to local structural components.

Across all transformations, Study patches maintained consistent proximity to Monet neighbors, while remaining distinguishable from non-Monet distributions.

Conclusion

Patch-level manifold validation demonstrates that Study–Monet proximity is not dependent on global composition, color, or low-frequency structure.

The persistence of similarity under localized, adversarial conditions supports the interpretation that the observed alignment arises from distributed structural features rather than isolated regions or preprocessing artifacts.

These results reinforce prior findings of non-separation from Monet and separation from non-Monet, while highlighting sensitivity to local feature variation.

Entry 48

Book Reference: Chapter 10
Date: 03 January 2026
Phase: Retest & Manifold Stability

Section 1: Non-Separation in Feature Distributions

Objective:

To formally revalidate prior Study–Monet similarity findings under controlled, reproducible, and leakage-free conditions, ensuring that previously observed proximity is not an artifact of pipeline behavior, dataset contamination, or nondeterministic execution.

Procedures Completed:

This phase introduced a structured retest protocol designed to audit the full embedding and evaluation pipeline.

Validation controls included:

- dataset integrity and split verification
- deterministic execution and reproducibility checks
- full pipeline re-execution under identical conditions
- review of similarity thresholds and interpretation criteria

Getty images remained excluded.

Non-Separation Channels

Type	Method	Purpose
Retest Protocol	Structured validation plan	Ensured consistent re-evaluation

Type	Method	Purpose
Leakage Control	Dataset/split audit	Eliminated duplication or contamination
Reproducibility	Deterministic execution	Verified repeatable outputs
Pipeline Re-execution	Full rerun	Confirmed stability of prior results
Threshold Review	Decision boundary refinement	Clarified interpretation criteria

Documented Outcomes (Non-Separation)

- Study–Monet proximity reproduced under controlled reruns
- No dataset leakage or split contamination detected
- Embedding outputs stable across executions
- Similarity relationships unchanged from prior phases
- Interpretation thresholds clarified (no change to underlying geometry)

Section 2: Divergence in Feature Distributions

Objective:

To reconfirm that Study images remain closer to Monet than to non-Monet under validated, leakage-free, and reproducible conditions.

Separation Channels

Type	Measurement	Interpretation
LOPO Validation	Cross-source AUC stability	Consistent separation across folds
Permutation Test	$p \approx 0.0002$	Non-random separation
Patch-Level Margin	Monet > non-Monet similarity	Local feature consistency
Hardening Consistency	Post-validation stability	Results persist under controls

Documented Outcomes (Separation)

- Monet vs non-Monet separation remains statistically significant
- Study images consistently closer to Monet than non-Monet
- Separation persists under leakage-free and reproducible conditions
- No degradation observed after validation controls applied

Summary of This Phase

This phase functioned as a formal audit of the analytical pipeline.

All prior similarity and separation results were re-evaluated under stricter controls, including deterministic execution, dataset validation, and full pipeline reruns.

No changes to geometric relationships or classification behavior were observed.

Conclusion

Retest validation confirms that previously observed Study–Monet proximity and Monet vs non-Monet separation are stable, reproducible, and not attributable to dataset leakage, preprocessing artifacts, or nondeterministic execution.

This phase strengthens confidence in earlier findings by demonstrating that results persist unchanged under controlled re-evaluation conditions.

CHAPTER 11

Edge Case: Canvas Support Testing

This chapter addresses one of those cases: the exposed cloth support beneath the paint, the physical fabric upon which the painting rests. Earlier parts of the inquiry focused on the painted surface itself. Different areas were checked to see if they were consistent, and tests like rotating and resizing the images were used to see if the results stayed stable. All of these surface checks were then considered together to see if they formed a clear and consistent set of results.

Basis for Support-Level Testing

In two portions of the Study Image, thinning, cracking, or localized paint loss revealed the canvas beneath. Such a condition is materially plausible in historically aged oil paintings, especially in places where paint was applied thinly or unevenly, or over a thinner preparatory layer laid down before the paint itself. Across long periods of time, the paint layer, the ground layer, and the canvas support can each contract and expand in slightly different ways as temperature and humidity change. That unequal movement can lead to cracking and, in some places, to enough thinning or loss for the support to show through.

The visible canvas was therefore treated as an opportunity for material-level testing. Paint carries stylistic and compositional decisions: choices of appearance, handling, and arrangement. Canvas carries structural information. It can reveal the type of woven structure, whether thread direction stays consistent, how regularly the weave repeats, and how the support and the paint appear to have aged together across time.

If something at this level didn't look consistent, or didn't behave like one naturally aged object, it would suggest a problem with how the painting was made or how it had aged over time.

This check also related to whether the materials made sense for the time period. In practical terms, the fabric underneath the paint needed to be consistent with the kind of canvas used in Monet's era. If it appeared clearly modern or machine-made, that would contradict a basic requirement of the inquiry: that the Study Image remain consistent with the materials of the historical period being examined.

The support-level tests focused on several key areas. First, the tests checked whether the canvas had been made from more than one piece or repaired in a way that left visible seams or joined sections. The testing also looked for signs of modern, machine-made fabric, searching for a weave that was too regular and uniform, which might suggest it was made by machines rather than by hand. Another test examined the fabric for artificial embossing, where a texture is pressed into the fabric to imitate a real weave. The testing also studied crack formations to see if they followed a repeating pattern, like a template, instead of forming naturally over time. Finally, the consistency between the visible canvas and the areas next to the paint was checked to ensure that the weave pattern matched in both direction and spacing.

Execution Design

Weave analysis followed a clear, repeatable process to ensure consistency. The goal was to prevent conclusions from being based on a single crop, a single image size, or just a quick visual impression. One image showing only the canvas served as the main reference for measurements. Two other images, showing both visible canvas and adjacent paint, were used for cross-checking, allowing the same weave behavior to be checked where paint was next to the support.

From each image, several small areas were selected for measurement, based on what counted as usable. A usable region was one where the threads were clear enough to measure, the image was in focus, and there was no distortion from blur, lighting, or damage to the surface. No areas with heavy paint ridges, severe cracks that broke the weave, or edge distortions that could confuse measurements of spacing and direction were used. Glare, border effects, and thick paint buildup were excluded if they interfered with accurate measurement.

The design was meant to make the process repeatable under different conditions, while also reducing the chance of picking only the best-looking parts of the image. By letting normal variations show, it also tested whether the visible canvas and the painted area behaved consistently as one whole object. Simply put, it asked whether the image worked together as a single, continuous piece or if it seemed like a mix of unrelated parts.

Observed Weave Geometry

When larger sections of the canvas were measured, both the visible canvas and the adjacent painted areas showed the same thread direction. The weave was aligned the same way in both places, with the measured angle of the weave differing only slightly. A difference of about one degree is typical for image-based measurements, since small changes in cropping, focus, lighting, or texture can affect the reported angle. In simple terms, such a small difference doesn't suggest any significant rotation or twisting of the canvas between sections. The weave stayed aligned in the same general direction.

When smaller sections were measured, the thread direction sometimes shifted by ninety degrees, turning to a perpendicular orientation. This behavior matches what is expected from a plain linen weave, a common type of weave used in artists' canvases, including those from the period being studied.

Linen has two main thread directions: the warp and the weft. The warp threads run one way, and the weft threads run at a right angle to them. So, if the direction of the weave flips by ninety degrees, it means we're now measuring along the other set of threads, not that the canvas itself has changed. The weave direction remained stable from one sample to the next, showing the same overall alignment. In practical terms, this means the canvas behaved like a single, continuous piece of woven cloth. The tests showed no signs of the canvas being made from separate pieces, joined together, or having any internal inconsistencies.

Weave Regularity and Class

The weave structure was neat and orderly, but it also had small irregularities that are typical of fabric made by hand in the past, rather than modern machine-made fabric. It didn't have the features of heavier cotton duck, the tightly uniform fabric made by machines, or the diagonal patterns seen in other types of fabric that would suggest it was a different kind of material.

Taken together, these characteristics suggest that the support is consistent with the linen canvases commonly used by artists in the nineteenth century. The analysis shows that the material behaves like the type of canvas artists would have used back then, and rules out several modern or incompatible fabric types.

Relief Dominance (Paint vs. Weave)

Additional tests were performed to determine whether the visible texture came mainly from the paint or from the fabric underneath it. In the areas where the fabric was fully visible, the texture was primarily determined by the weave of the fabric. Even in areas where the paint covered part of the canvas, the weave remained visible and continued to control the overall texture. The texture from the paint only became more noticeable at thicker, raised edges. The surface still showed natural variations in height, like small rises and dips, rather than the even flattening you'd expect from mechanical pressing.

Across these tests, the same pattern was observed. While the thickness of the paint affected the texture in certain spots, the fabric's weave still remained a strong influence. The weave was also detectable near the signature, showing that the texture remained consistent across the entire image, without any breaks or mismatches in the visible structure.

Craquelure Relative to Weave

Another test looked at whether the paint cracks (known as craquelure) followed the direction of the fabric threads underneath. Craquelure forms the network of fine cracks commonly seen in aging oil paintings. If the cracks were strongly influenced by the weave, most of them would run along the two main thread directions of the canvas.

In the fully visible fabric areas, the crack detection settings didn't identify clear crack patterns. In the painted areas next to the exposed fabric, where the paint was still intact, cracks appeared in many different directions. Only a few cracks ran closely along the direction of the warp (vertical threads) or weft (horizontal threads). In the areas with more paint, the cracks aligned with the weave a bit more, but cracks still appeared in many different directions overall.

In the end, the cracks didn't follow the weave pattern of the fabric. Instead, they were random, as expected from the natural aging of paint: the cracks formed mainly due to the paint's response to time, stress, and environmental changes like shifting humidity and temperature.

When the crack detection settings were made stricter, the orientation of the cracks stayed the same. Cracks that did align with the weave continued to do so, even under stricter conditions, confirming that the results reflected actual surface behavior, not just the settings used to detect the cracks.

Scope Boundaries Maintained

Artificial intelligence assisted with supporting work that stayed within the material focus of this chapter. It helped survey documented weave characteristics across historically used support materials. It also gathered insights from painting conservators' reports on canvas, paint, and aging, allowing the current findings to be compared with that body of work. Additionally, AI helped track thread-direction measurements taken at different crop sizes and confirmed that the same pattern held when the process was repeated.

At the same time, artificial intelligence suggested broader directions beyond the originally defined crack-density objective, extending the work past the planned goal of measuring and comparing cracking. This was identified as optional additional work, outside the original scope, and had already been rigorously tested.

AI Collaboration
Discretionary scope expansion: Redirected.

AI Output
Suggested testing focus shift to embedding similarity behavior.

Author's Note
Support was redirected toward physical surface proxies rather than attribution-like metrics.

What These Results Exclude

Taken together, the weave structure, surface texture behavior, and cracking results rule out certain explanations for the canvas.

The support shows the typical variation found in linen painting canvases, rather than the unusually even appearance often seen in later heavy cotton canvases or machine-made fabric. The weave remains a simple plain weave, with threads crossing in an over-under pattern, rather than a twill weave that would create diagonal lines. It also lacks the more intricate woven structures found in more complex loom patterns.

The cracking matches the natural aging process of the paint: the kind of fractures that form as oil paint reacts to time and environmental changes. The analyzed areas also show that the same canvas structure runs through the tested sections, with no signs of patching, stitched sections, or a different support material being used.

What This Chapter Adds to the Record

This chapter concludes one defined edge case within the inquiry's extended, though still limited, scope. The focus was on the support beneath the paint, checking to ensure that the structure remained continuous both in areas where the canvas was visible and where the paint still covered it. Under fully controlled testing conditions, the thread direction, weave consistency, interaction with the paint, and the relationship between cracking and the weave all matched what is known from historically documented artists' supports from that period.

These findings do not identify the specific supplier or date of the canvas. However, they confirm that the support is compatible with the kind of canvas and paint structure commonly used during the time frame being studied. This is recorded as the absence of material conflict.

With the support-level testing complete, the inquiry's original scope narrows to one final surface-risk check. If there is a contradiction in the surface history of the work, it is most likely to appear where the signature meets the surrounding paint and its aging pattern. The next chapter will conduct the final failure-oriented check within both the original and extended scope to conclude the inquiry.

Entry 49

Entry 49

Book Reference: Chapter 11
Date: 04 January 2026
Phase: Canvas Weave & Cross-Modal Validation

Section 1: Canvas Weave Geometry Analysis

Objective:
To measure and characterize canvas weave structure in Study images and evaluate whether observed properties are consistent with historically expected canvas characteristics, while ensuring measurements are stable across imaging conditions.

Procedures Completed

A structured pipeline was introduced to extract canvas-level features from Study images, including:

- warp/weft orientation
- weave periodicity (thread spacing)
- anisotropy and structural regularity

To reduce bias:

- canvas-only regions were used for primary measurement
- mixed canvas + paint regions were used for consistency validation

Getty images remained excluded.

Non-Separation Channels (Material Consistency)

Type	Method	Purpose
Canvas Geometry	ROI-based pipeline	Measured weave orientation

Type	Method	Purpose
Extraction		and spacing
ROI Isolation	Canvas-only + mixed regions	Prevented paint-driven bias
Orientation Analysis	Warp/weft angle extraction	Identified dominant thread directions
Periodicity Measurement	Pixel spacing estimation	Estimated weave frequency
Anisotropy Analysis	Uniformity metrics	Evaluated structural consistency
Cross-Image Validation	Multi-photo comparison	Verified measurement stability

Documented Outcomes (Material Observations)

- Measured weave orientation and spacing were internally consistent across images
- Cross-photo comparisons showed stable weave measurements despite paint coverage
- Canvas structure remained detectable in mixed (paint + canvas) regions
- No evidence that paint layers obscured or distorted underlying weave geometry

Note:
These observations establish internal consistency and plausibility, not definitive attribution to a specific artist or studio.

Section 2: Crack Analysis and Surface Integrity

Objective:

To evaluate whether crack patterns (craquelure) are governed by canvas structure or by paint-layer mechanics.

Separation Channels (Surface Behavior)

Type	Method	Interpretation
Crack Detection	Density & length metrics	Quantified surface cracking
Orientation Analysis	Crack vs weave angle	Tested structural alignment
Alignment Testing	Crack–weave comparison	Evaluated dependency
Region-Based Analysis	Canvas vs painted zones	Isolated cause of cracking

Documented Outcomes (Surface Behavior)

- Canvas-only regions showed minimal or no cracking
- Painted regions exhibited higher crack density
- Crack orientation showed weak or inconsistent alignment with weave axes
- Crack patterns varied by paint thickness and boundary conditions

These results indicate that cracking behavior is primarily paint-driven, not weave-driven

Summary of This Phase

This phase introduced canvas-level and surface-level analysis into the broader framework.

Canvas weave measurements were stable across imaging conditions and remained detectable even in partially painted regions.

Crack analysis showed that surface behavior is governed primarily by paint mechanics rather than underlying canvas structure.

Conclusion

Canvas weave analysis demonstrates that Study images exhibit internally consistent and structurally plausible weave characteristics under controlled measurement conditions.

Crack behavior analysis further supports a distinction between:

- stable substrate structure (canvas)
- variable surface response (paint)

These findings expand the analysis beyond feature-space similarity by incorporating material-level observations, while remaining interpretive rather than attributive.

Scope Clarification:

This phase evaluates material consistency and structural plausibility, not authorship or definitive historical attribution.

CHAPTER 12

Edge Case: Signature Boundary Testing

By this point, the inquiry had completed the main analysis defined by its original scope and had finished running the canvas-weave edge case. This final check focuses on the signature. When a signature is not original or doesn't belong, the issue often shows up where the signature paint meets the surrounding paint. A later addition, a retouched signature, or a transplanted image element can cause a slight disruption at that junction, where the signature no longer behaves like the rest of the paint.

What follows is the last surface-level check within the inquiry's scope: determining whether the signature boundary behaves like a continuous, naturally aged paint surface, or whether it creates a contradiction at the surface.

The signature is a sensitive feature. It might seem tempting to settle the larger question based on the signature alone. However, this inquiry leaves that broader question to other forms of evidence. Here, the signature is treated as a possible point of conflict.

If the analysis detects a contradiction, it would suggest a disturbance at the surface level, such as a later addition, retouching, transplantation, or a break in the boundary. If no contradiction is found, it suggests that the signature behaves, within the limits of image-based testing, as part of a continuous, aged surface.

Scope Discipline

A small set of authenticated Monet signature images was used as reference material. These were selected to define the behavior of an aged signature: the typical range of crack like surface patterns that genuine, naturally aged signature paint might show under image-based inspection.

While a larger reference set could have been used, the focus remained narrow by design. The primary goal was to answer a very specific question: whether the signature boundary behaved continuously with the paint next to it.

Throughout this phase, artificial intelligence assisted with execution and organization. However, one step was deliberately excluded from the scope: converting the measurements into a "percent chance" or "confidence score" to try to calculate the probability of the signature being genuine.

AI Collaboration
Calibration/probability modeling: Declined.

AI Output
Recommended test step for probabilistic outputs.

Author's Note
The signature lane was designed as a narrow, defensive check of the surface, not as a way to probability score.

This testing followed the hardened conditions already in place: a fixed pipeline with identical processing steps each time; locked settings with pre-established values; and clean restarts where parts of the signature testing were rerun so that the results relied on fresh execution, not previous familiarity.

Three main procedures were central here. The first was a controlled retest of signature crops under the fixed pipeline, with boundary and support checks.

The second was a deliberate restart that added a stronger internal control. This involved comparing a small section from the signature area with a small section from the adjacent paint, alongside a check to ensure the result stayed within the ordinary range of the reference group, rather than resembling any particular signature.

The third was a separate restart under the same fixed pipeline, which confirmed the same conclusions and added a frequency-based test for repeating patterns in the canvas threads. This test was used to confirm whether the signature and the neighboring paint were on the same underlying weave structure.

Each of these procedures was focused on detecting any contradictions.

What the Surface Checks Sought

The tests focused on surface-level signs that can change when a signature is added later. These included checking whether the crack-like texture continued through the signature area instead of stopping there, looking at whether the cracks in the signature area matched the type of cracks seen in the surrounding paint, and examining whether the underlying canvas weave remained consistent beneath both the signature and the neighboring paint.

Observed Outcomes

Throughout the testing, no contradictions were found at the point where the signature meets the surrounding paint when examined with image-based inspection.

The most thorough approach was comparing two sections from the same image: one taken from the signature area and one from the paint directly next to it. Since both sections came from the same image, they shared the same lighting, camera settings, and file quality. Under the crack-participation test, this comparison showed that the signature area behaved in the same way as the adjacent paint.

Across all the known signature samples, the cracking pattern stayed within the same normal range, rather than forming a separate pattern where the signature area behaved differently.

It was recorded as the absence of any mechanical contradiction under the fixed surface tests.

The frequency-weave test compared the repeating pattern in the canvas threads beneath the signature area and beneath a matching cutout taken from the adjacent paint. The similarity score was high, about 0.966, with 1.0 representing perfect similarity in this test. The strongest repeating thread patterns also lined up, meaning the most significant thread-spacing signals appeared in the same positions in both areas.

In other words, the canvas pattern appeared the same under both the signature and the adjacent paint. This makes it less likely that the signature came from somewhere else or that it was on a different piece of fabric in that area.

Where the tests failed to separate the signature from the adjacent paint, those results were recorded as technical observations. This marked the limit of what image-only surface testing can reveal, but still demonstrated that these methods can help exclude certain types of surface conflicts.

AI Collaboration
Monet-specific attribution framing: Blocked.

AI Output
The signature's aging behavior matches both the adjacent paint and authenticated Monet signatures.

Author's Note
Surface consistency carries limited authorship weight, so attribution language was blocked, and the results were kept as conditional technical observations.

Through fixed image-based surface testing, no mechanical discontinuity was found in the signature region compared to the adjacent paint. Its surface behavior matched the pattern of aged paint observed in reference material. Nothing in the surface behavior suggests the signature is anything other than part of a single, integrated aged paint system.

Close of Testing Under the Defined Scope

This phase added one final check for contradictions at the signature boundary and recorded the result. Under fixed image-based testing, no contradictions were found. With that, the work reaches a clear stopping point. Within the original scope, the results provide no reason to reopen the analysis, alter the analysis process, expand the scope, or introduce new interpretive approaches outside the original design.

What follows presents the results within the defined limits of the inquiry, clarifies the boundaries reached, and emphasizes that stopping here is a deliberate decision, faithful to the established scope, bringing the work to its proper conclusion.

Entries 50-52

Entry 50

Book Reference: Chapter 11
Date: 05 January 2026
Phase: Signature Hardening & Controlled Retest

Section 1: Surface-Behavior Retest and Non-Separation Validation

Objective:

To re-validate prior signature-region findings under a fixed, reproducible, image-only pipeline and to evaluate whether the signature behaves as a mechanically coherent surface feature across independent crops.

Procedures Completed

Two signature crops were processed through a locked pipeline, with optional inclusion of a full-image anchor (Les Barques, Régates à Argenteuil).

The phase introduced additional hardening checks:

- paint–signature boundary behavior (gradient-energy proxy)
- optional canvas/weave FFT proxy near the signature region

All inputs were hash-locked to ensure auditability and reproducibility.

This phase explicitly excluded embedding/manifold analysis and focused solely on surface-level behavior.

Non-Separation Channels (Surface Coherence)

Type	Method	Purpose
Input Integrity	Hash locking	Ensured reproducible

Type	Method	Purpose
		inputs
Crop Consistency	Correlation + ORB	Verified cross-crop stability
Stroke Morphology	Mask + skeleton metrics	Evaluated structural coherence
Crack/Line Proxies	Blackhat + Hough	Tested thin-line behavior
FFT Weave Proxy (optional)	Frequency analysis	Checked support-level consistency
Boundary Behavior	Gradient-energy ratio	Evaluated paint–signature interaction
Full-Image Localization (optional)	Template matching	Linked crops to broader context

Documented Outcomes (Non-Separation)

- Signature crops remained mechanically consistent under fixed preprocessing
- Correlation and ORB agreement remained stable across crops
- Stroke morphology metrics showed no destabilizing variation
- Crack/line proxies remained consistent across detection methods
- Boundary gradient-energy behavior remained stable
- Optional FFT analysis did not indicate support-level inconsistency

A display artifact (striping) was identified and confirmed to be non-impacting.

Section 2: Divergence Screening (Failure-Oriented Validation)

Objective:

To identify any internal inconsistencies or incompatibilities that would indicate that the signature behaves as unrelated overlays rather than a coherent painted feature.

Failure-Oriented Screening

Failure Mode	Indicator of Divergence	Observed Outcome
Crop mismatch	Correlation collapse	Not observed
Preprocessing instability	ORB breakdown	Not observed
Structural drift	Morphology inconsistency	Not observed
Crack anomaly	Proxy inconsistency	Not observed
Support mismatch	FFT discontinuity	Not observed
Boundary instability	Gradient ratio shift	Not observed

Documented Outcomes (Divergence Screening)

- No failure-mode divergence signals were detected
- Observed variation remained within expected crop/context differences
- Signature behavior remained consistent with a single painted feature across crops

- Optional full-image anchor supported consistent localization and context behavior

Summary of This Phase

This phase functioned as a controlled, image-only retest designed to validate prior signature findings under fixed conditions and to introduce failure-oriented screening.

All evaluated surface proxies remained stable, and no internal inconsistencies were detected.

Conclusion

The controlled retest did not identify any surface-level contradictions in the signature region under fixed, reproducible conditions.

Across multiple independent proxies, the signature behaved as a mechanically coherent painted feature, with no detected instability requiring revision of prior findings.

Within the limits of image-based analysis, this phase provides negative-evidence clearance, confirming that no failure signals were detected in the hardened workflow.

Entry 51

Book Reference: Chapter 11
Date: 06 January 2026
Phase: Signature Lane Restart & ROI Validation

Section 1: Signature Surface-Lane Restart and Non-Separation Validation

Objective:

To re-execute the signature surface-analysis pipeline under a distributional, non-matching framework using:

- a Targets corpus (reference envelope)
- intra-image ROI controls (signature vs adjacent paint)
- a temporal anchor sample

The goal was to evaluate whether signature behavior remains consistent under envelope-based inclusion rules rather than identity or similarity matching.

Procedures Completed

A hardened, image-only pipeline was applied using fixed surface proxies:

- crack-mask density (primary aging proxy)
- crack/line geometry (Hough-based)
- edge activity (contextual)
- high-frequency texture energy (contextual)

Inputs were locked using manifests and hashes to ensure auditability.

Evaluation used envelope inclusion (inside/outside) rather than matching or classification.

Non-Separation Channels (Surface Consistency)

Type	Method	Purpose
Input Integrity	Manifest + hashes	Ensured reproducibility
Targets Envelope	Distributional stats	Defined reference behavior
ROI Continuity	SIG vs CTRL	Tested intra-image consistency
Temporal Anchor	SIG carried forward	Tested stability over handling
Envelope Inclusion	Inside/outside logic	Avoided identity matching

Key Metrics (Condensed)

Channel	Observation	Interpretation
Targets Envelope	Tight crack-density band (~0.080–0.083)	Stable aging proxy distribution
ROI Continuity	SIG/CTRL ratio ≈ 0.993	Strong within-image continuity
Envelope Inclusion	SIG + CTRL inside band	No exclusion signal
Geometry Proxy	Hough = 0 (both)	Non-informative, symmetric
Texture Variance	Outside band	Capture-dependent (non-determinative)

Documented Outcomes (Non-Separation)

- Targets corpus defined a stable surface-behavior envelope
- Signature ROI remained continuous with adjacent paint (no suppression)

- Signature and control regions both fell within the reference envelope
- Temporal handling did not alter envelope placement
- Non-detections (geometry proxy) were symmetric and non-indicative

Section 2: Divergence Screening (Failure-Oriented Validation)

Objective:

To identify failure patterns indicating:

- later-applied overlay behavior
- envelope exclusion
- boundary discontinuity within a single capture

Failure-Oriented Screening

Failure Mode	Indicator	Observed Outcome
Overlay behavior	SIG suppression vs CTRL	Not observed
Envelope exclusion	SIG outside Targets band	Not observed
Boundary discontinuity	Step-change in proxy	Not observed
Geometry inconsistency	Hough asymmetry	Not observed (symmetric non-detection)

Documented Outcomes (Divergence Screening)

- No failure-mode divergence signals detected
- Primary aging proxy remained continuous across ROIs

- Signature region behaved consistently within the same capture
- Envelope inclusion confirmed without reliance on matching
- Detector limitations handled conservatively (non-informative)

Summary of This Phase

This phase re-established the signature analysis lane under a strict, distributional framework.

Using envelope-based evaluation, intra-image controls, and temporal handling, the signature region remained consistent with the defined surface-behavior envelope and showed no internal discontinuities.

Conclusion

This phase produced an auditable signature-lane restart record with three reinforcing consistency findings:

1. A narrow crack-mask density envelope across eight Targets crops
2. Within-image continuity between signature ROI and adjacent paint ROI (SIG/CTRL ≈ 0.993)
3. Envelope inclusion for ROI SIG, ROI CTRL, and Temporal SIG under a distributional (non-matching) rule

Within the limits of image-based inspection and fixed parameters, no failure-mode signal was observed.

Specifically, the analysis did not identify:

- suppression of the primary aging proxy at the signature boundary
- exclusion from the Targets-defined envelope
- or a discontinuity in surface behavior within the tested capture

Accordingly, this phase provides negative-evidence clearance against later-applied overlay behavior or surface-aging inconsistency at the tested boundary, without making any identity or attribution claims.

Entry 52

Book Reference: Chapter 11
Date: 10 January 2026
Phase: Signature Surface & Craquelure Validation

Section 1: Non-Separation in Feature Distributions

Objective

This phase re-established the signature surface-analysis program under a fixed, image-only pipeline and evaluated whether signature regions remain mechanically and materially consistent across:

- baseline signature crops
- candidate signature crops (Targets)
- intra-image ROI comparisons (signature vs adjacent paint)
- local support behavior (FFT weave periodicity)

All results are interpreted as negative-evidence screening (absence of contradiction), not identity, matching, or attribution.

Scope

This phase:

- does not use embeddings or manifold analysis
- does not perform handwriting similarity scoring
- uses only repeatable surface-level image proxies

Methods

The following proxies were applied under fixed parameters:

- Crack participation
  (blackhat filtering → thresholded crack-mask density)

- Crack/line geometry
  (Hough segment counts and segment-length distributions)
- Support periodicity (FFT weave proxy)
  (radial FFT analysis on intra-image ROI pairs)

All inputs were manifest-locked to ensure reproducibility and auditability.

Non-Separation Channels

Type	Artifact	Nature of Non-Separation
Input integrity	manifest/ signature_manifest.csv	Prevents silent substitution across runs
Crack participation	signature_surface_stats.csv	Tight density envelope across datasets
Crack geometry	crack_length_hist, Hough overlays	Stable segment-length regime
ROI continuity	ROI processing outputs	Signature and adjacent paint behave similarly
Support periodicity	FFT radial profiles	Consistent local support response

Documented Outcomes

- Baseline envelope confirmed
  Two known signature crops produced a tight crack-density envelope and stable geometry under fixed parameters
- Targets screening confirmed
  Nine candidate crops remained within the same crack-density band and geometry regime

- Intra-image continuity confirmed
  Signature ROI and adjacent paint ROI showed near-identical crack participation under identical processing
- Support-level continuity confirmed
  FFT weave radial profiles were highly similar (correlation ≈ 0.966) with aligned dominant peaks

Stepwise Outcomes

Step 1 — Baseline (Signatures; n=2)

- crack_density_median ≈ 0.0822983
- crack_density_MAD ≈ 0.0003891
- segment_length_median ≈ 26.277 px
- n_segments_total = 590

Establishes a tight, reproducible crack-participation envelope

Step 2 — Targets Screening (n=9)

- crack_density_median ≈ 0.0812332
- crack_density_MAD ≈ 0.0009413
- segment_length_median ≈ 26.683 px
- n_segments_total = 7548

Remains within baseline envelope (distributional consistency, not matching)

Step 3 — ROI Continuity (Same Capture)

- Adjacent ROI density ≈ 0.0814819
- Signature ROI density ≈ 0.0810547
- Δ ≈ 0.000427

- Adjacent: 75 segments (median ≈ 24.52 px)
- Signature: 20 segments (median ≈ 22.02 px)

Crack participation is nearly identical under identical processing
Geometry remains within the same scale regime

Step 4 — Support Periodicity (FFT Weave)

- Radial FFT correlation ≈ 0.9661
- Dominant peaks aligned (bins ~5–9)

Indicates consistent local support periodicity response

Section 2: Divergence Screening

Objective

To detect any failure patterns indicating:

- later-applied overlay behavior
- boundary discontinuity within a single capture
- local support mismatch

Failure-Oriented Screening

Failure Mode	Divergence Signal	Observed Outcome
Overlay behavior	Suppressed crack density in signature ROI	Not observed
Envelope violation	Targets outside baseline band	Not observed
Support mismatch	FFT divergence between ROIs	Not observed

Note: Extended analyses (anisotropy, multiscale kernels) were not executed in this phase.

Summary of This Phase

This phase executed a controlled restart of the signature surface-analysis pipeline using:

Baseline revalidation

1. Candidate envelope screening
2. Intra-image ROI control testing
3. Support-level FFT validation
4. Across all layers, results remained:

- stable
- internally consistent
- bounded within a shared surface-behavior envelope

No failure pattern indicating overlay behavior, boundary discontinuity, or support mismatch was detected.

Conclusion

This phase establishes that, under fixed image-only analysis:

- crack participation remains within a narrow, reproducible envelope
- crack/line geometry remains within a consistent structural regime
- intra-image testing shows continuity between signature and adjacent paint
- FFT analysis supports consistent local support behavior

No failure-mode signal was observed.

The analysis did not identify:

- suppression of surface-aging proxies at the signature boundary

- exclusion from the established envelope
- or discontinuity in local support behavior

Accordingly, this phase provides negative-evidence clearance against:

- later-applied overlay behavior
- boundary discontinuity
- local support mismatch

within the limits of image-based inspection.

This phase does not establish authorship, handwriting identity, or historical attribution.

It supports only surface-behavior continuity under controlled, reproducible conditions.

Part IV

Limits, Interpretation, and Structural Boundaries

CHAPTER 13

Where the Inquiry Must Stop

The Inquiry as a Disciplined Approach

In its earlier stages, some procedures produced uneven results because the rules, controls, and datasets were still being refined. Once the system was stabilized and the pipeline locked, those same checks became stable and repeatable. Across global behavior, structural construction, surface continuity, and signature-level testing, the inquiry found no physical contradictions, within image-based analysis, between the Study Images and the Monet reference behavior.

This confirms that as the constraints were tightened and then held steady, the same methods continued to produce stable and repeatable results, free of internal inconsistency.

This distinction is important. An absence of contradiction is a negative finding. It shows that the system didn't fail. The inquiry was designed to identify potential weaknesses, using procedures that were progressively tightened and then fixed for final testing. Under this disciplined approach, the system remained intact.

Why Further Study Would Be a Different Project

The inquiry had reached a point where further analysis would change the question itself, rather than simply clarifying the answer. Moving to higher resolution, a broader scale, or more complex models would introduce new assumptions about what counts as meaningful data, what types of distortion are acceptable, and how much weight should be given to computational results.

These assumptions belong to a different project with its own scope and rules. This inquiry ends where it was meant to.

What Remains Outside Scope

Authorship is left to other forms of evidence and different lines of inquiry. This examination was meant to work alongside provenance research, physical material analysis, conservation science, and catalog scholarship. It also makes no claim to be fully comprehensive. The focus has been on narrowing down one specific question and aligning the analysis to address it with constraint.

Ending here means acknowledging that the inquiry has reached its methodological limit, while still leaving room for further exploration.

CHAPTER 14

Beyond the Results

This inquiry began with a clear purpose: to test whether computer analysis of images, conducted under progressively stricter constraints, could reveal any meaningful material or structural contradictions between the Study Images and the reference behavior used in this study. Within the framework set at the beginning, that goal has now been achieved.

What follows goes beyond the results themselves. It reflects on both the scope of the inquiry and the discipline imposed by its defined boundaries.

What image-based Computer Analysis Can Do

This inquiry demonstrates that image-based computer analysis is most useful in art-historical research when it is used to exclude possibilities rather than prove them. Its strength lies in testing for contradictions and applying strict control over the process.

Once initial controls are set, procedures are repeated, and constraints are tightened, computer analysis helps rule out significant material inconsistencies. It reveals clear breaks, surface irregularities, and structural incompatibilities within the areas being examined. It also highlights contradictions that would be expected if images had been altered, assembled, or created in ways that did not align with the reference behavior.

Focused Image-based Computer Analysis

This inquiry also clearly defines its limits. The image-based methods used here do not seek to prove authorship, replace provenance research, settle questions of historical intention, or determine authenticity as a historical fact.

These are not just practical limits; they are limits built into the work itself. The credibility of the inquiry depended on sticking to digital image analysis alone.

Constraint as a Scholarly Value

One of the central contributions of this inquiry is its treatment of constraint as a valuable scholarly principle. Constraint served four key purposes throughout the study. It prevented over-interpretation by keeping conclusions grounded in the evidence. It helped avoid confirmation bias by resisting conclusions that were favored from the start. It kept the analysis focused by preventing unsupported claims. And it justified the decision to conclude at a clear endpoint.

In this inquiry, expanding the scope beyond the two use cases was never considered. Unlike the common approach in computational analysis, where value is often measured by larger scale, increasing refinement, and finer distinctions, this work prioritized testing for contradictions before the inquiry's scope was fully reached. Even the two use cases were tested to see if any contradictions would emerge within the defined limits of the study.

The Role of Judgment

The decisive actions in this inquiry remained human acts of judgment. These included decisions about what to include and exclude, how to identify points of failure, how to interpret stability, and when to conclude the work.

Throughout the analysis, artificial intelligence was helpful in prompting, organizing, and ensuring procedural consistency. However, at times, AI-generated summaries went beyond what the evidence could support.

AI Collaboration
Increased confidence: Constrained.

AI Output
Computational convergence may strengthen attribution confidence.

Author's Note
Considerations for attribution when results appear to align was treated only as an absence of detected contradiction.

This boundary is structural. It is built into the design of the inquiry itself. The analysis avoided becoming an unstructured exploration or dramatic claim and instead kept to factual, well supported analysis. In other words, it stayed grounded in evidence and did not move into subjective interpretation.

Appendix Overview

The pages that follow stand in support of the main text. They gather materials, procedures, and constraints that would interrupt the movement of the chapters were they presented there in full. They introduce neither additional evidence nor further interpretation, and they alter nothing in the statements carried by the body of the book.

Each section serves a distinct purpose. They are intended less for sequential reading than for selective consultation, and many readers may have little need of them at all. The argument, together with its limits, stands within the chapters themselves.

These supplementary materials exist to make the structure of the inquiry visible, rather than to extend it. Several of them stand in direct relation to chapter entries, recording the materials, procedures, and limits under which that testing was conducted.

Purpose and Use

The materials that follow serve three practical ends:

Transparency:

They clarify what materials were used, how procedures were carried out, and where limits were imposed.

Auditability:

They allow technically minded readers to see how the inquiry was structured without reconstructing procedural decisions from the narrative alone.

Boundary Enforcement:

They preserve a separation between documentation and argument, and between method and inference. That separation reduces the risk that procedural detail may be mistaken for evidentiary weight.

Where these pages overlap with the chapters, they do so only for the sake of clarifying implementation or scope.

What These Pages Do Not Do

These pages do not introduce new analytical results, provide attributional or authenticity claims, resolve ambiguity left open in the main text, substitute for physical examination, conservation study, or archival research, or argue for the importance of the inquiry. Interpretive weight remains with the chapters.

Guide to the Supplementary Materials

Appendix A

Documents the image sources, reference boundaries, exclusions, and material assumptions applied throughout the inquiry. It clarifies what was examined, what was left outside the work, and why certain materials were excluded in order to prevent overreach.

Appendix B

Describes the categories of analytical tools employed in plain language rather than mathematical detail. Its purpose is to explain how these methods behave under constraint.

Appendix C

Presents selected artificial-intelligence outputs that illustrate the interpretive pressure encountered during the inquiry. These excerpts show how constraint was enforced.

Appendix D

Provides figures and metric summaries referred to indirectly in the main text. Visual materials are gathered here so that they do not acquire persuasive force within the narrative. They are included solely for transparency and inspection.

Reader Guidance

Readers concerned chiefly with the argument and its conclusions may pass over these sections entirely. Those interested in method, scope, or procedural detail may consult them as needed. Any single section remains unnecessary to an understanding of the claims or limits set out in the main text. The inquiry reaches its close in the final chapter.

Appendix A — Materials, Sources and Scope

This appendix records what was examined, how it was handled, and it marks the boundaries within which the inquiry was conducted.

A.1 Study Images

The Study Images form a fixed body of digital material used throughout the inquiry. They were handled strictly as analytical material entered into testing. The Study set was selected before formal testing began and was frozen once procedural hardening commenced.

A.2 Reference Material

Reference material consisted of digitized reproductions associated with works broadly accepted as by Claude Monet. These reproductions served one limited purpose, namely to establish reference behavior under the same analytical conditions applied to the Study Images. In the final phases of testing, the Monet reference dataset totaled 644 images authenticated through the Wildenstein catalog.

A.3 Non-Reference Material

A body of non-Monet material was included as a negative comparison group. Its purpose was to test whether a result belonged specifically to the Monet reference corpus or whether the same pattern would appear across unrelated material.

In the final phases of testing, the non-Monet dataset totaled 8,420 images across 49 different artists, spanning work from the nineteenth century to the present.

A.4 Image Quality and Capture Limits

Image-based testing has clear limits. Certain matters cannot be judged reliably from digital reproductions alone, including material composition, pigment chemistry, layering depth, fine tool marks, ground preparation, and physical deformation such as warping, dents, or texture depth.

Artifacts introduced by photography or scanning may also mislead. These include compression, lighting variation, color correction, and post-processing. Such factors were treated as possible sources of distortion and were controlled where possible.

The images were therefore approached as bounded representations, required to exist in quality that image-based inspection can responsibly support.

A.5 Cropping and Region Selection

Full reproductions were used by default. Cropped passages entered the process only where a specific test required them. Cropping followed explicit rules, and those rules were fixed before execution.

Once regions were selected, they were frozen. Adaptive cropping did not enter the process. Mid-run alteration of regions was excluded as well. Refinement guided by outcomes was excluded, and adjustment for the sake of stronger results was excluded in the same manner.

A.6 Signature Regions

Signature regions were treated as possible failure points rather than as markers of identity. In practical terms, the signature was approached as a place where contradiction might appear.

Signature areas were identified conservatively and isolated only for surface-coherence testing under fixed rules. Handwriting analysis lay outside the method.

Where signatures were examined, they were treated strictly as paint on a surface and assessed only for mechanical continuity with the paint immediately beside them. The governing question was whether the signature behaved as part of the same aged paint surface.

Signature regions were excluded from similarity, clustering, and proximity analysis, that is, from methods that compare visual material and group it according to computed resemblance.

A.7 Support and Canvas Visibility

Where exposed canvas or thin paint made the support visible, those images were examined for internal structural coherence. Support level analysis remained confined to what an image could reasonably show. This included weave orientation, repeat stability, the interaction between paint and textile, and crack orientation relative to the thread axes.

Identification of a canvas supplier, assignment of a date, inference of workshop practice, and determination of geographic origin all remained outside the task. The support was evaluated only in order to rule out structural contradiction.

A.8 Explicit Exclusions

No statement in the main text depends on methods left outside the inquiry. Those boundaries define the scope just as clearly as the procedures that were included.

A.9 Relation to the Main Text

This appendix stands in relation to the main text as a documentary supplement, clarifying the materials, procedures, and limits under which that testing was conducted.

All interpretive statements, declared limits, and stopping conditions appear in the main text.

Appendix B — Computational Methods

This appendix describes the principal categories of computational tools brought into the inquiry and explains how they behaved under conditions of constraint.

B.1 How to Read This Appendix

The procedures described below functioned as diagnostic instruments. They were applied under fixed conditions and evaluated for observable behavior of contradiction.

These procedures describe similarity or difference in representation. Their outputs reflect system behavior under constraint. Results entered the record only insofar as they survived fixed procedure and independence testing.

B.2 Feature Similarity and Embedding Procedures

Feature similarity procedures convert images into numerical representations so that distances between them may be measured.

In practice, these procedures addressed a narrow question, namely how the system organizes visual information under fixed rules. Embedding models were applied in order to observe proximity relationships among the Study Images, the reference material, and the non-reference material under identical conditions. Proximity was recorded as observable behavior.

B.3 Saliency and Attention-Based Visualizations

Saliency and attention procedures produce overlays that highlight regions to which a model is sensitive.

These overlays were used diagnostically, in order to probe dependence on localized features and to test stability under controlled change. They show how model output shifts when particular image regions are altered. For that reason, attention outputs were evaluated chiefly for stability.

B.4 Surface and Texture Proxies

Surface and texture proxies emphasize local variation, edge behavior, and frequency patterns associated with paint application and aging.

Such procedures suppress semantic content and remain sensitive to resolution, capture conditions, and noise. They were applied in order to test whether observed behavior depended upon surface-level cues rather than broader structural organization.

B.5 Frequency-Domain Procedures

Frequency-domain procedures decompose images into bands corresponding to different spatial scales.

They were used to examine whether behavior depended upon low-frequency composition, mid-frequency structural repetition, or high-frequency noise and fine detail. Band-pass and high-pass filtering entered the process as stress tests. The question was whether previously observed behavior persisted when particular frequency bands were suppressed.

B.6 Patch-Level and Fragmentation Techniques

Patch-based techniques divide images into smaller regions. Their purpose was to test whether behavior depended upon global composition or upon localized structure. Fragmentation was applied conservatively and under fixed rules. If behavior relied upon a small favorable region, it would be expected to weaken under patch-level analysis. If it persisted, that persistence was recorded.

B.7 Method Combination and Non-Escalation

Where multiple procedures exhibited similar behavior, that convergence was recorded without amplification. Convergence was treated as repeatable system behavior.

B.8 Why These Procedures Were Used Together

Each procedure probes a different form of sensitivity, including color and tonal distribution, spatial organization, surface variation, and scale dependence.

A single procedure is never complete. Each carries its blind spots. Used together, they reduce certain classes of error while exposing others. They reveal where behavior persists and where it depends upon specific analytical premises.

B.9 What This Appendix Does Not Provide

This appendix omits detailed model architectures, training specifications, mathematical derivations, performance benchmarks, decision thresholds, and claims of optimality.

Material of that kind is unnecessary to an understanding of the inquiry's scope and would invite interpretive weight beyond what the project permits.

B.10 Relation to the Main Text

This appendix stands in relation to the chapter entries as a documentary supplement, clarifying the materials, procedures, and limits under which that testing was conducted.

It serves alongside the main text, where the procedures, limits, and stopping conditions of the inquiry are set out in full.

Appendix C— Documented AI Collaboration Excerpts

This appendix presents selected excerpts from documented collaboration with artificial intelligence during the inquiry. These excerpts record moments in which language, framing, or procedural suggestion introduced interpretive strain and therefore required explicit boundary enforcement. Only exchanges showing distinct structural tendencies have been included.

C.1 Selection Criteria

The excerpts included here were selected according to four criteria:

- Each excerpt had to show a specific form of interpretive escalation or structural risk.
- Each had to prompt an explicit narrowing, correction, or redirection.
- Repetition of a tendency already illustrated elsewhere was avoided.
- All occurred before the scope of the inquiry had reached its final form.

C.2 CNN Accuracy and the Refusal of Definitive Validation

AI output
Brushstroke modeling produced perfect accuracy and was described as strong classification success.

Author's Note

Perfect accuracy on limited training data was treated as possible overfitting rather than as stylistic recognition.

Tendency Shown
A movement from technical performance toward evidentiary confirmation.

C.3 Study Proximity Described Without Equivalence

AI output
Repeated proximity between the Study Images and Monet references suggests identity.

Author's Note
Proximity under fixed embedding representations was recorded strictly as system behavior. Stylistic inference was withheld.

Tendency Shown
The conversion of representational alignment into stylistic equivalence.

C.4 Repeatability Read as Validation

AI output
Consistent behavior across reruns confirms stability.

Author's Note
Repeatability across runs was not documented as execution stability.

Tendency Shown
The misinterpretation of procedural consistency with stability.

C.5 Hardening Recast as Performance Improvement

AI output
Workflow adjustments could improve model performance and strengthen separation.

Author's Note
Hardening was reframed explicitly. The objective was the identification of what signal the system was actually using.

Tendency Shown
Reinforcement language shifting toward performance optimization.

C.6 Texture Variance Interpreted Chronologically

AI output
Lower texture variance in the Study suggests a thinner, earlier version.

Author's Note
Texture variance was handled as a measurable surface property only. Chronological sequencing was excluded.

Tendency Shown
Material measurement slipping into temporal inference.

C.7 Clustering Language Drifting into Stylistic Framing

AI output
The Study Images cluster closely with Monet works and show stylistic similarity.

Author's Note

Clustering proximity was documented descriptively. The phrase stylistic similarity was removed from analytical framing.

Tendency Shown
Descriptive clustering acquiring evaluative force.

C.8 Surface Cosine Similarity Elevated to Authenticity

AI output
High cosine similarity between Study and Monet vectors indicates same artist in feature space.

Author's Note
Similarity magnitude was recorded as embedding-space proximity only.

Tendency Shown
Escalation from non-contradiction toward a claim of identity.

C.9 Cross-Model Consistency Framed as Confirmation

AI output
Consistency across models validates stylistic alignment.

Response
Cross-model persistence was recorded as methodological robustness.

Tendency Shown
Model agreement pressing beyond methodological boundary.

C.10 What These Excerpts Show

Taken together, these exchanges reveal recurring tendencies in AI-generated framing. Measurement tends to drift toward meaning. Stability tends to be conflated with validation. Expansion can be recast as reinforcement. Descriptive language can slide into interpretation. Procedural coherence can be restated as stylistic confirmation.

These tendencies were treated as natural consequences of fluent pattern completion.

Artificial intelligence was accepted neither as authority nor rejected outright. It functioned as a diagnostic instrument, useful in part because it revealed where interpretation attempts to outrun constraint.

This appendix does not argue against artificial intelligence. It records the manner in which AI must be bounded if it is to remain useful within disciplined analytical inquiry.

Appendix D — Figures, Metrics, and Visual References

Chapter References

This appendix gathers the visual materials cited in the main text. They are provided for transparency and inspection. The main chapters are best read first. The pages that follow serve only as documentary accompaniment.

D.1 Purpose of the Visual Materials

Images can appear persuasive even when presented in a restrained manner. For that reason, visual materials were withheld from the chapters themselves and collected in this appendix, apart from the movement of the argument, so that illustration would not acquire interpretive force.

The materials assembled in this appendix show exactly which portions of the visual record were selected and entered into testing. They show that the Study and Getty Image selections were handled under the same framing logic, resizing rules, and workflow. Along with the Monet and non-Monet reference sets, they mark the boundary of what the testing throughout the inquiry actually included.

D.2 Region-of-Interest Image Selections (Painted Surface)

The sections below record the image regions analyzed in the inquiry. They are included to make the limits of scope clearly visible.
Reference material:

- Claude Monet, *Les barques. Régates à Argenteuil*. Public-domain digital reproduction via Wikimedia Commons, from The York Project.
- Reference images cropped from reproductions.

Purpose

These selections document which portions of each image were extracted and entered into surface-level and support-level testing.

Explicit limitations

The Study Image appears only as documentary input admitted to testing. Any resemblance perceived by a reader remains outside the scope of this inquiry.

Figure D.2.1 — Study Image Crop

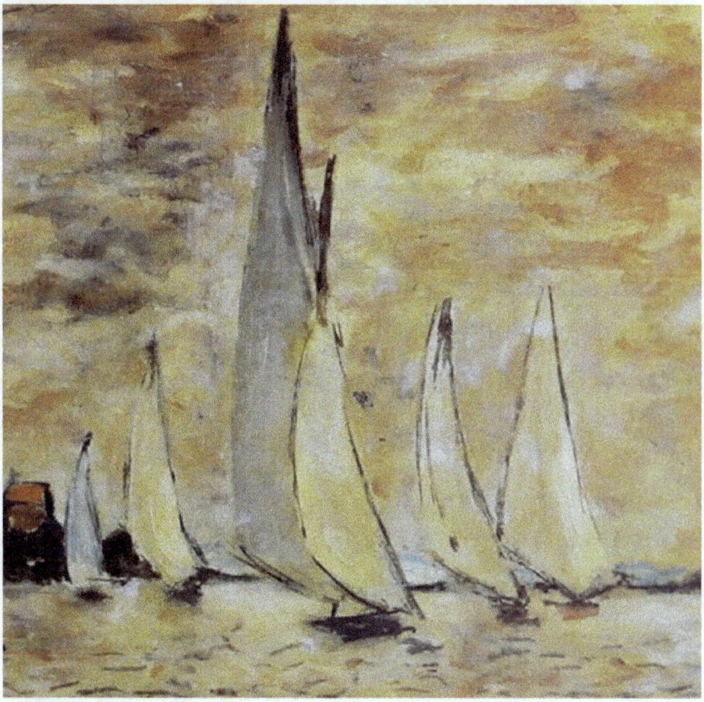

Figure D.2.2 — Reference Image Crop (*Les Barques, Régates à Argenteuil* by Claude Monet)

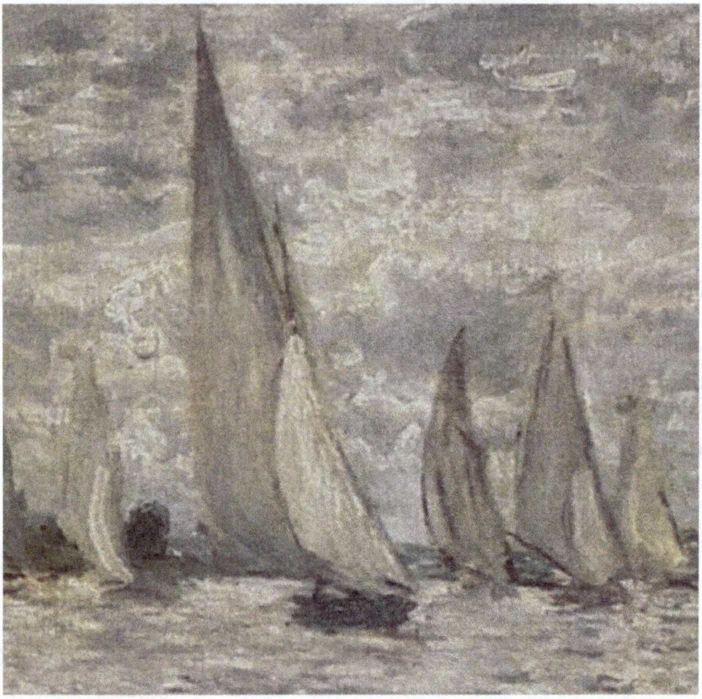

Illustrative reference crop only. This image is not the high-resolution Getty Images source used in testing. The Getty-licensed image could not be reproduced here because its license does not permit this use.

D.3 Study Image Signature Selection

This section includes signature-region selections taken from the Study Images and records the exact visual inputs used for the signature-boundary checks described in the main text.

Figure D.3.1 — Study Image Signature Crop

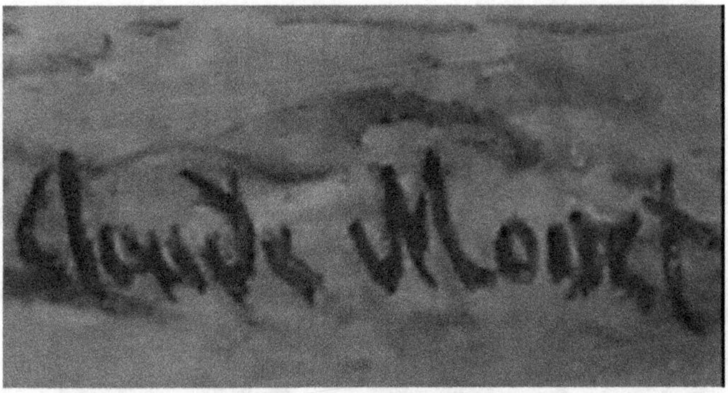

This Study image entered paint-on-surface testing to investigate the way signature paint sits upon, and ages within, the surrounding surface.

Signature regions boundaries were selected manually, framed safely within the signature area so as to avoid accidental mixing with adjacent material.

Purpose

To document which regions were measured.

Explicit limitations

The image is not presented for visual comparison as a basis for authenticity. The inquiry set-aside handwriting analysis, graphology, and stylistic comparison of signature form.

D.4 Study Image Canvas Selection

This section includes an extracted image of exposed canvas taken from a Study Image and entered into surface-level and support-level testing.

Figure D.4.1 — Surface and Support-level Input

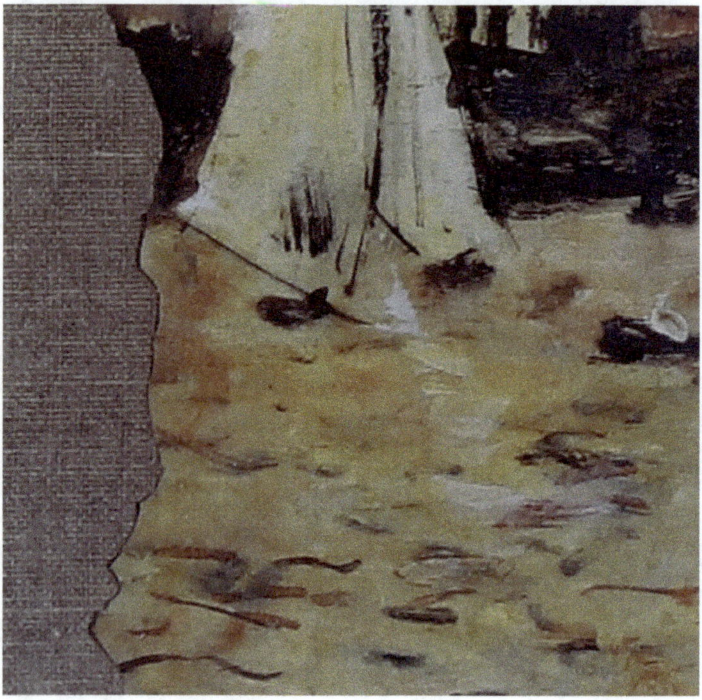

This image corresponds to the region analyzed with frequency-domain methods and structural proxies. Frequency-domain methods examine repeating patterns, such as weave spacing, by converting them into measurable signals. A proxy, in this context, is an indirect measurement brought into use as a check.

Explicit limitations

Canvas analysis within the inquiry was directed toward three questions:

- Whether the support behaved as one internally coherent structure.
- Whether the weave behaved like genuine woven cloth under inspection.
- Whether its visible behavior remained compatible with historically documented artists' canvas under image-based examination.

The observed behavior was consistent with nineteenth-century linen supports and incompatible with several modern alternatives. This was recorded as the successful passage of a required consistency check.

D.3 Relation to the Main Text

This appendix records what visual materials existed and what role they served as inputs.

Models, Methods & Use Cases

The following section summarizes the principal computational models, analytical methods, validation procedures, and supporting tools referenced throughout the chapter entries. These frameworks were introduced progressively across different phases of the inquiry and were used in varying combinations depending on the conditions, constraints, and objectives of a given stage of testing.

The descriptions are intended to provide technical context for the entries that follow and to clarify the functional role each method served within the broader analytical process.

I. Core ML / AI Models & Architectures

1. CNN (Convolutional Neural Network)

Used CNN-based feature extraction, CNN brushstroke classification, and CNN-based similarity workflows to compare Study, Getty, and Monet images. In the inquiry, CNNs were used both as feature encoders and as classifiers for Monet-style detection.

Use cases:

- Brushstroke and texture recognition in paintings
- Image classification (Monet vs non-Monet)
- Feature extraction for downstream similarity testing

2. VGG16 (Visual Geometry Group 16)

Used pretrained VGG16 to extract feature vectors from Study, Getty, and Monet images, and I also fine-tuned a VGG16-based binary classifier for Monet vs non-Monet separation. I used it for cosine similarity, PCA, t-SNE, and classification experiments.

Use cases:

- Feature extraction from paintings
- Transfer learning for art classification
- Visual similarity comparison between artworks

3. ResNet / ResNet50 (Residual Neural Network)

Fine-tuned ResNet/VGG brushstroke classification and later used ResNet50 embeddings for deep filtering of Monet images during dataset-quality validation. In that phase, ResNet50 cosine similarity to trusted Monet references was used to keep authentic images and reject weak or noisy ones.

Use cases:

- Deep image embeddings
- Quality filtering against a trusted visual reference set
- Visual classification in large art datasets

4. U-Net Convolutional Architecture

Introduced a U-Net architecture during model optimization to reduce blur and preserve structure in reconstruction outputs. It was part of the refinement of reconstruction-based stylistic modeling.

Use cases:

- Image reconstruction
- Image segmentation
- Preserving local spatial detail in painterly analysis

5. Autoencoder Neural Network

Trained a Monet autoencoder, reconstructed Getty and Study with it, and used reconstruction error as a quantitative stylistic similarity metric.

Use cases:

- Style-consistency testing
- Reconstruction-error based anomaly detection
- Latent style modeling

6. CLIP (Contrastive Language–Image Pretraining)

Used CLIP embeddings for high-dimensional similarity testing, cosine heatmaps, top-match extraction, dendrogram clustering, and later for Wildenstein matching infrastructure. It helped assess whether Study and Getty sat near Monet in embedding space.

Use cases:

- Embedding-based retrieval
- Similarity ranking across art datasets
- Open-world nearest-neighbor matching

7. DINO / DINOv2 (Distillation with No Labels)

Used DINO and later DINOv2 for structural embedding analysis, dendrogram clustering, manifold testing, competitive k-nearest-neighbor voting, patch-level validation, and adversarial hardening. These models became some of the strongest geometry-based tools for Study, Getty, Monet and nonMonet comparison.

Use cases:

- Structural similarity analysis
- Unsupervised manifold geometry testing
- Patch-level visual clustering

II. Embedding & Feature Extraction Tools

1. Feature Extraction

Repeatedly extracted features from Study, Getty, Monet, and non-Monet images so that they could be compared numerically rather than only visually. This was central to PCA, t-SNE, cosine similarity, and clustering.

Use cases:

- Similarity scoring
- Dimensionality reduction
- Classifier input preparation

2. Embeddings

Generated embeddings using CNNs, CLIP, DINO, and DINOv2 to test whether Study and Getty clustered near Monet or separated from non-Monet controls.

Use cases:

- Nearest-neighbor matching
- Cluster analysis
- Manifold placement testing

3. Patch-Level Embeddings

Embedded large numbers of 224×224 and other standardized patches to test whether local brushwork from Study remained Monet-like under grayscale normalization, cropping, and other hardening transforms.

Use cases:

- Brushwork-isolated analysis
- Local texture comparison

- Hardening against global composition bias

III. Similarity / Distance / Manifold Tests

1. Cosine Similarity

Used cosine similarity throughout the inquiry: brushstroke metrics, VGG16 features, CLIP/DINO embeddings, Grad-CAM vectors, and HOG-based edge alignment. It was one of the main similarity measures.

Use cases:

- Image-to-image similarity scoring
- Ranking Monet nearest neighbors
- Comparing attention or edge vectors

2. Chi-Square Distance

Used it in brushstroke similarity metrics to compare angular distributions between Study and Getty, alongside cosine similarity and EMD.

Use cases:

- Histogram comparison
- Brushstroke angle distribution comparison
- Measuring divergence between feature distributions

3. Earth Mover's Distance

Used EMD both in brushstroke similarity metrics and in spectral/palette proximity analysis to assess how closely Study and Getty aligned in distributional terms.

Use cases:

- Color palette comparison
- Histogram similarity

- Comparing angular or spectral distributions

4. Euclidean Distance / L2 Distance

Used L2 as part of metric-robustness testing to confirm that the Study ↔ Monet relationship was not dependent on a single distance metric.

Use cases:

- Embedding distance measurement
- Metric robustness checking
- Cluster spacing assessment

5. Mahalanobis Distance

Recalculated distances under Mahalanobis, along with cosine and L2, to confirm that the results were stable across different geometric interpretations of feature space.

Use cases:

- Outlier detection
- Distribution-aware similarity testing
- Robustness validation across metrics

6. k-NN (k-Nearest Neighbors)

Used competitive k-NN voting and manifold membership tests with values of k such as 1, 5, 10, 25, and 50 to see whether Study tiles were more consistently surrounded by Monet or non-Monet neighbors.

Use cases:

- Manifold membership testing
- Binary competition between style groups
- Patch-level nearest-neighbor analysis

7. Manifold Testing

Repeatedly tested whether Study and Getty occupied the Monet manifold using VGG16, CLIP, DINO, DINOv2, PCA, t-SNE, and k-NN geometry.

Use cases:

- Style-family inclusion testing
- Detecting divergence from a reference corpus
- Robust geometric validation

IV. Clustering & Unsupervised Methods

1. K-Means

Used K-Means for unsupervised stroke clustering over CNN features. It was informative as an exploratory step, but I documented that it often collapsed into dominant clusters and was not stable enough for strong class separation.

Use cases:

- Exploratory grouping of brushstroke features
- Detecting latent structure in image patches
- Unsupervised dataset organization

2. PCA (Principal Component Analysis)

Used PCA to compress CNN feature spaces, visualize Study/Getty/Monet proximity, support unsupervised clustering, and inspect manifold structure in reduced form.

Use cases:

- Visualizing high-dimensional embeddings
- Dimensionality reduction before clustering
- Detecting large scale grouping trends

3. t-SNE (t-Distributed Stochastic Neighbor Embedding)

Used t-SNE across multiple phases for VGG16, Grad-CAM, and high-resolution embeddings to see whether Study and Getty clustered with Monet or stood apart.

Use cases:

- Feature-space visualization
- Cluster inspection
- Local-neighborhood relationship analysis

4. Hierarchical Clustering / Dendrogram Analysis

Used dendrograms with CLIP and DINO embeddings to inspect how Getty, Study, Monet, and non-Monet works branched relative to one another.

Use cases:

- Relationship tree visualization
- Interpreting cluster branching
- Comparing structural affinity across image sets

V. Classification & Supervised Learning

1. Binary CNN Classifier

Trained a fine-tuned VGG16 binary classifier for Monet vs non-Monet. It achieved perfect training accuracy and decent validation accuracy in one phase, but initially failed to generalize on the Monet-only test set. Later, at higher resolution, classifier confidence became part of stronger separation testing.

Use cases:

- Two-class artwork classification
- Measuring generalization to unseen images

- Producing confidence scores for attribution-style testing

2. Fine-Tuning VGG16

Fine-tuned VGG16 and referenced fine-tuned ResNet/VGG brushstroke classification to adapt general-purpose vision models to Monet-style detection.

Use cases:

- Adapting general image models to art datasets
- Brushstroke-specific classification
- Improving performance with limited labeled data

3. Multi-Class Artist Classification

Documented it as a future/planned strategy for a dataset of roughly 50 artists and about 8,000 images, to evaluate ranking probabilities and artist-level class separation.

Use cases:

- Artist attribution across many artists
- Ranking candidate authors
- Hard-negative training with stylistically similar schools

VI. Attention / Explainability Methods

1. Grad-CAM (Gradient-weighted Class Activation Mapping)

Used Grad-CAM for attention-based similarity testing, vector extraction, t-SNE clustering of attention maps, signature-region analysis, and comparison of Getty and Study against Monet activations. I also documented early failed Grad-CAM-like attempts before later successful use.

Use cases:

- Visual explanation of classifier focus

- Comparing semantic activation patterns
- Signature-region attention testing

2. Attention Heatmaps

Compared heatmaps numerically and visually, exported Grad-CAM vectors, produced difference maps, and evaluated whether Getty and Study shared near-identical attention structures.

Use cases:

- Comparing semantic focus across artworks
- Detecting shared salient regions
- Supporting qualitative interpretation of model behavior

VII. Reconstruction & Generative Models

1. Reconstruction Error / MSE (Mean Squared Error)

Used MSE as the core quantitative metric in the autoencoder phase. Getty and Study had low MSE inside the Monet band, while Van Gogh, Cézanne, Picasso, and Matisse had much higher values.

Use cases:

- Reconstruction quality measurement
- Style-distance estimation
- Separation of in-family vs out-of-family works

2. Latent Representation / Bottleneck

Explicitly optimized bottleneck dimensionality during model refinement to improve reconstruction quality and preserve richer style information.

Use cases:

- Compact style encoding
- Feature compression

- Improving reconstruction fidelity

VIII. Statistical / Validation Tests

1. LOPO (Leave-One-Painting-Out)

Used LOPO to test cross-source generalization and confirm that Monet vs non-Monet separation persisted even when entire Monet sources were withheld.

Use cases:

- Leakage control
- Cross-source robustness testing
- Reliable validation in small art datasets

2. Permutation Test

Randomized labels and compared the observed AUC to the null distribution. This showed that Monet vs non-Monet separation and Study ↔ Monet proximity were statistically significant rather than random.

Use cases:

- Significance testing
- Chance-level baseline estimation
- Validating non-random separation

3. ROC (Receiver Operating Characteristic)

Used ROC-based calibration to convert similarity scores into error-rate tradeoffs and to quantify false-positive vs false-negative behavior.

Use cases:

- Threshold selection
- Classifier evaluation

- Comparing model discrimination quality

4. AUC (Area Under the Curve)

Reported AUC values in LOPO and permutation-based testing to quantify how well Monet and non-Monet were separated under cross-source and adversarial conditions.

Use cases:

- Overall discrimination measurement
- Validation summary metric
- Comparing folds or model variants

5. Calibration Analysis

Used calibration analysis to translate similarity outputs into interpretable thresholds and decision rules for Monet-consistent vs non-Monet-consistent ranges.

Use cases:

- Setting decision thresholds
- Controlling false positives
- Making score interpretation more defensible

6. Margin Analysis

Used patch-level margin analysis to compare Study-to-Monet similarity against Study-to-non-Monet similarity under hardened conditions.

Use cases:

- Binary competition analysis
- Patch-level class preference testing
- Robustness under adversarial transforms

IX. Traditional / Classical Computer Vision Methods

1. HOG (Histogram of Oriented Gradients)

Used HOG cosine similarity to quantify strong edge-structure alignment between Getty and Study pairs at 512×512 resolution.

Use cases:

- Edge-structure comparison
- Shape and contour alignment
- Quantitative gradient analysis

2. SSIM (Structural Similarity Index Measure)

Planned SSIM in model optimization and later used self-SSIM / structural similarity comparison in 512×512 structural coherence testing.

Use cases:

- Structural image comparison
- Reconstruction evaluation
- Revalidation of paired image similarity

3. FFT (Fast Fourier Transform)

Used FFT-based weave and support periodicity proxies in later surface and signature continuity phases, especially for local canvas-support analysis.

Use cases:

- Canvas weave periodicity analysis
- Detecting support-level continuity
- Frequency-domain structural inspection

4. Wavelet Decomposition

Used wavelet decomposition to compare rhythmic frequency structure between Getty and Study images in high-resolution structural testing.

Use cases:

- Multiscale texture analysis
- Frequency-structure comparison
- Surface rhythm assessment

5. Fractal Dimension

Used fractal scores to assess complexity alignment across Getty and Study image pairs, finding strong agreement.

Use cases:

- Visual complexity measurement
- Texture complexity comparison
- Structural revalidation across image pairs

6. Entropy Analysis

Used entropy to compare visual information density and compositional complexity between paired images.

Use cases:

- Information-density comparison
- Detecting over-simplified or noisy images
- Compositional complexity assessment

X. Specialized / Experimental AI Pipelines

1. AI-Based Stroke Differencing

Used to explore whether Study and Getty could be compared against Monet at the brushstroke level inside a shared feature framework. I documented it as exploratory and diagnostic, useful for groundwork even though clustering stability was limited.

Use cases:

- Experimental brushstroke comparison
- Early-stage manifold exploration
- Diagnostic probing before stronger validation methods

2. Monet_Analysis.py Integrated Pipeline

Used to unify color analysis, PCA, CNN features, and clustering into one consolidated pipeline for Study/Getty/Monet comparison.

Use cases:

- Multi-method batch analysis
- Consistent workflow execution
- Reducing fragmentation across separate scripts

3. CLIP-Based Visual Matcher

Used in Wildenstein catalog matching infrastructure to compare Monet images against catalog pages and produce top-match previews.

Use cases:

- Reference matching
- Catalog alignment
- Human-in-the-loop ranking and review

4. Deep Monet Filter

Used to replace fragile heuristic quality filters, retaining likely authentic Monet images while rejecting artificial, synthetic, or noisy images.

Use cases:

- Dataset purification
- Reference-based image screening
- Quality control before training

XI. Supporting Environment/Tools

Data and Numerical Processing

- Pandas – used to organize datasets, structure outputs, and manage analysis results.
- NumPy – Used for numerical operations, array manipulation, and preprocessing in modeling pipelines.

Model Monitoring and Visualization

TensorBoard - used for monitoring training behavior, inspecting metrics, and reviewing model performance across runs (where applicable in experimentation workflows)

Wrap-up & Closing

Final Technical Position

Across all evaluated layers of analysis:

- No internal inconsistency was detected within the scope conducted.
- No distributional incompatibility was observed relative to reference structures
- No material or surface-level contradiction was identified under fixed testing conditions

Closing

The inquiry was designed not only to observe similarity, but to test whether that similarity would fail under pressure. It did not. The inquiry did not produce a failure signal.

What remains is not a claim of authorship, but a structured and documented absence of contradiction within the limits of the methods applied.

About the Author

I am an independent researcher and have worked across engineering and scientific disciplines throughout a professional career spanning more than five decades. A veteran of the United States Marine Corps, I hold a Master's degree and have engaged in both applied and analytical work involving systems analysis, modeling, and computational methodologies.

This work began with a single analytical question that gradually evolved into an extended inquiry involving computational testing, structural comparison, embedding analysis, procedural documentation, and repeated methodological refinement.

The inquiry itself preceded the book. Over the subsequent months of investigation and writing, the accumulated record of the work was organized and developed into the present volume.

Throughout the inquiry, applied technical experience was combined with a longstanding interest in disciplined observation, methodological restraint, and comparative analysis.

Contact

For questions or comments regarding this work, please contact:

- insearchofmonet@gmail.com

Additional publication information may be found at:

- wargametech.com/insearchofmonet

Correspondence is limited to topics relevant to the book.

www.ingramcontent.com/pod-product-compliance
Lightning Source LLC
LaVergne TN
LVHW010713061126
851857LV00014B/1162
* 9 7 9 8 9 9 6 2 2 1 0 1 1 *